Contents

New Testament Social Ethics for Today

Richard N. Longenecker

GRAND RAPIDS, MICHIGAN
WILLIAM B. EERDMANS PUBLISHING COMPANY

To Beth and Lawrence,
with love!

Copyright © 1984 by William B. Eerdmans Publishing Co.
255 Jefferson Ave. S.E., Grand Rapids, Michigan 49503
All rights reserved
Printed in the United States of America

Library of Congress Cataloging in Publication Data

Longenecker, Richard N.
    New Testament social ethics for today.

    Bibliography: p. 99
    1. Bible. N.T.—Hermeneutics. 2. Sociology, Biblical.
3. Ethics in the Bible. I. Title.
BS2331.L66 1984   241   84-1663

ISBN 0-8028-1992-3

PREFACE

The content of this little book stems from four lectures I gave on "The Relevance of New Testament Social Ethics for Today" at the Wycliffe College Clergy School during November 1979. In whole or in part, I then used the material in a number of study sessions at various Anglican, Baptist, and Presbyterian churches in the Toronto area, and I presented abridged portions of it at various learned society meetings in North America. I also presented the material in a lectureship sponsored by Inter-Varsity at Lakehead University, Thunder Bay, Ontario, in October 1981; as the Nils W. Lund Memorial Lectures at North Park Theological Seminary, Chicago, Illinois, in October 1982; and as the Fall Lectures at Ashland Theological Seminary, Ashland, Ohio, in October 1983.

I've learned much from all who have written on the subject (see footnotes and bibliography) and from those who interacted with the presentations in public sessions. In effect, I've "stood on the shoulders" of many, and I thank you all!

RICHARD N. LONGENECKER

INTRODUCTION

For the majority of Christians, the significance of the New Testament for social ethics is a subject shrouded in mystery and clouded with uncertainty. Personal ethics, it is often assumed, are another matter, for that is what the Bible is all about, and human nature has remained essentially the same from antiquity to the present. But of what use, it is asked, are the ideas and solutions of the writers of the New Testament for contemporary social issues when society has changed so dramatically and situations are not at all the same? For most Christians the maxim seems to be this: Follow the personal ethics of the New Testament as far as circumstances allow, yet realize that we live in an immoral society and that therefore some compromises must be made in the realm of human affairs.[1]

A large part of our confusion regarding Christian social morality stems from our uncertainties regarding the place of the New Testament in forming a Christian social consciousness and its function in the expression of such a consciousness. How should the New Testament be used in the various areas of social concern? Of what relevance are its statements, principles, and practices for us today? These are matters having to do principally with hermeneutics—the art and science of interpretation, particularly biblical interpretation. And these are the questions this book is concerned with.

But before getting into the subject directly, a few words should be said about the book's title, for it was chosen with a view to saying something about my purposes and procedures in writing. First, then, as for the word "relevance"—

[1]This is a caricature of Reinhold Niebuhr's *Moral Man and Immoral Society* (New York: Scribner's, 1934).

which is unspoken but certainly implied: it suggests *an apologetic purpose*. No doubt the word has been overused and so devalued. More importantly, many modern "history of religion" approaches to biblical study have disputed the legitimacy of attempting to derive norms from the Bible for either Christian belief or Christian behavior.[2] Yet following out a modified "salvation history" approach—one which takes seriously the descriptive emphasis of a history-of-religions approach but also believes the New Testament to be the touchstone for Christian thought and life today—it will be my purpose in what follows to argue that any system of social morality which claims to be Christian must be informed by the New Testament, and that the New Testament has much to teach us regarding social thought and practice today.

The debate between scholars of a purely history-of-religions stance (where attention is devoted exclusively to the critical and historical study of primitive Christianity) and scholars espousing a salvation-history approach (where the results of that descriptive study are held to be in some way normative for the formulation of contemporary Christian doctrine and practice) is particularly heated today.[3] It is impossible here to attempt any theoretic resolution. All I can hope

---

[2]Wilhelm Wrede's *Über Aufgabe und Methode der sogenannten neutestamentlichen Theologie* (Göttingen: Vandenhoeck & Ruprecht, 1897) was probably most significant in establishing this approach. The stance is continued in Jack T. Sanders' *Ethics in the New Testament: Change and Development* (Philadelphia: Fortress Press, 1975) and Dennis Nineham's *The Use and Abuse of the Bible* (London: Macmillan, 1976). In discussing "whether and to what degree an Occidental of the modern day may look to the New Testament for any guidance or clues for behavior" (*Ethics in the New Testament*, p. xi), Sanders concludes: "The ethical positions of the New Testament are the children of their own times and places, alien and foreign to this day and age. Amidst the ethical dilemmas which confront us, we are now at least relieved of the need or the temptation to begin with Jesus, or the early church, or the New Testament, if we wish to develop coherent ethical positions. We are freed from bondage to that tradition and we are able to propose, with the author of the Epistle of James [citing Jas. 2:15–16], that tradition and precedent must not be allowed to stand in the way of what is humane and right" (p. 130).

[3]James M. Robinson, in "The Future of New Testament Theology," *Religious Studies Review*, 2 (January 1976), 17–23, discusses the debate from a history-of-religions perspective; Reginald H. Fuller, in "What is Happening in New Testament Studies?" *Saint Luke's Journal of Theology*, 23 (1980), 90–100, discusses it from a salvation-history stance.

is that, in what follows, my proposed developmental hermeneutic, my exposition of the New Testament's ethical proclamation, and my treatment of Christian practice as recorded
in the New Testament and the pages of church history will
provide justification for the approach I am taking—and, more
importantly, will impress on the reader the relevance of the
New Testament's ethical proclamation and practice for contemporary Christian living.

By speaking in the title of "New Testament" social ethics,
rather than simply "Christian" social ethics, I am attempting
to highlight *a hermeneutical purpose* which seeks to show how
the New Testament should be understood and used in areas
of social concern. Admittedly, a discussion of New Testament
social ethics is narrower in scope and more limited in detail
than that of "Christian social ethics." But I have chosen to
write a work dealing principally with hermeneutics, and so
I am content to hold myself mainly to the New Testament
materials and only to point to some implications for life today.

Some of my readers will suggest that I should speak more
broadly of "biblical" social ethics and so include more overt
reference to the Old Testament. But while happily acknowledging continuity between the Old and New Testaments, and
while often attempting to demonstrate that continuity in what
follows, in my proposed developmental hermeneutic I focus
on the canonical New Testament as the touchstone for Christian faith and life, and so my argument must begin there.[4]
Others will object that because of diversity within the early
Church it is wrong to take the canonical writings as such a
touchstone, and that because of diversity within the canonical
writings themselves it is illegitimate to speak of a New Testament view of anything—particularly of such an abstract idea
as "New Testament social ethics." I agree that it is important
to recognize the diversity within both early Christianity generally and the New Testament in particular. Yet it remains true
that it was the twenty-seven books of our New Testament
which were brought together by the early Church to be the

---

[4]With such an emphasis on both continuity and development, I declare
myself to be in line with the Antiochian Fathers—not Marcion (who argued
for discontinuity) and not the Alexandrian Fathers (who proposed a static
sameness in the Testaments).

authoritative expression of the Christian religion, with their diverse treatments serving to enhance the fullness of the revelation that came in Jesus Christ, and their commonly held "sense of center" (to use James Moffatt's phrase) highlighting what should be considered normative for all succeeding Christian thought and action.

Obviously, it is vital to include "social ethics" in the title, because the subject matter is what the New Testament presents by way of proclamation and practice regarding Christians and society. Here, of course, I have *a didactic purpose*, for only as there is a faithful exposition of the material will there be engendered insights into and conviction regarding the relevance of the subject for our present day. Granted, life can never truly be separated into so-called personal and social dimensions. Yet for purposes of analysis, such dimensions can be identified and treated somewhat separately. And it is just such an analysis of the New Testament materials on the subject of Christians in society that seems particularly appropriate in our day.

Finally, the inclusion of the word "today" in the title signals *a hortatory purpose*. Taking the New Testament's own "wherefore-therefore" style of exposition and application as my example, I purpose in what follows to exhort to an obedient response and to urge an appropriate action. The hortatory features of this work I find personally to be most disconcerting, for the material strikes home constantly by way of rebuke and challenge. But a didactic purpose without an accompanying hortatory purpose would be in any salvation-history approach a perversion of scholarship—and, more importantly, for any Christian (I believe) a truncating of the gospel. So I confess both my pain and my joy in treating this aspect of the study, trusting that my readers will experience something of the same.

Of course, much that should be said on so important a topic will remain unsaid or be dealt with in far too cursory a fashion in so brief a work as this. What follow are not all-inclusive expositions but paradigm studies. The first two chapters deal with the hermeneutics of New Testament social ethics, laying out a proposal for understanding and implementing the proclamation and practice contained within the

New Testament. The third, fourth, and fifth chapters build on statements in Galatians 3:28 that express the cultural, social, and sexual mandates of the gospel, showing how they were understood and worked out in the early Church, and pointing toward how they should be applied today. The epilogue highlights the relevance of the material for today, dealing with challenges and prospects. While the chapters are paradigmatic in nature, it is hoped that they will provide a new way of understanding the New Testament on social ethics, offer greater insight into what Christian social ethics are all about, and challenge us all to greater social responsibility as Christians.

NEW TESTAMENT
SOCIAL ETHICS
FOR
TODAY

I. An Initial Dilemma:
To Whom Shall We Go?

Christians generally have accepted the New Testament as their guide for faith and life. But Christians vary widely in their beliefs as to how the New Testament should be used in moral theory and practice. Often we are like the disciples of old who cried out in their confusion: "Lord, to whom shall we go?" (John 6:68). Most Christians, in fact, come up short at the very beginning of their attempt to think and act "Christianly" in areas of social morality, unable to decide how the New Testament should guide them in doing so. And being thwarted here, they become catatonic ethically. It is therefore necessary in this first chapter of our discussion to look at various ways in which the New Testament has been understood as a guide to Christian morality, then to highlight certain basic features of a biblical ethic that say something about how we should resolve our hermeneutical dilemma, and, finally, to propose a working solution as to how the New Testament should be used in moral theory and practice. In the next chapter I will focus the hermeneutical issues more specifically by proposing a developmental schema for understanding New Testament social ethics.

A. FOUR WAYS OF USING THE NEW TESTAMENT

Broadly speaking, there are four ways in which Christians use the New Testament in ethical decision-making and practice. Each has its own advocates, who generally are so enamored with their own approach that they identify it alone as worthy of the name "Christian." Yet each position needs to be set out

1

and evaluated so that we might be better able to make a proper start in our ethical thought and action.

The first of these positions is that which takes the New Testament as a book of laws or a summation of codes for human conduct. It argues that God has given prescriptive laws in the form of commandments and ordinances, which can be found in both the Old and the New Testaments. If people want to know what they should do, the laws of God stand objectively before them in written form, and they have only to refer to them. This was the ethical approach of Rabbinic Judaism, which came to systematic expression in the Halakic codifications of the Mishnah, the Tosephta, the Palestinian and Babylonian Gemaras, the "Sayings" collections of individual ancient rabbis, Rashi's commentary on the Talmud, and Maimonides' 613 commandments. It is also the attitude of many fervent Christians today, whether they focus narrowly on the teachings of Jesus or on the letters of Paul, take into account the entire New Testament, or include the broader spectrum of both Old and New Testaments.

The truth of such a position lies in the fact that the words of Jesus and the statements of the New Testament writers are given with prescriptive force and do not come to us as tactical suggestions. Jesus reaffirmed such Old Testament commands as those having to do with loving God (cf. Mark 12:29–30, par.; quoting Deut. 6:4–5), loving our neighbors (cf. Mark 12:31, par.; quoting Lev. 19:18), honoring our parents (cf. Mark 7:10; Matt. 15:4; quoting Exod. 20:12; 21:17), and the indissolubility of marriage (cf. Mark 10:7–8; Matt. 19:5; quoting Gen. 2:24). Matthew's Gospel, in fact, portrays Jesus as in some sense a new Lawgiver (especially chapters 5–7), and John's Gospel presents him as speaking of his teachings as commandments and as commending obedience to his words (cf. 13:34; 14:15, 21; 15:10, 12). Throughout the New Testament, as also in the Old Testament, the divine will is set forth as that which is objective to all human calculations and normative for every human activity. In the later Pauline and Petrine epistles, in fact, the Christian religion is depicted in terms of a new law (cf. the use of "commandment" in 1 Tim. 6:14 and 2 Pet. 2:21).

Yet the Gospels also proclaim Jesus as being much more

than a Moses *redivivus*, and the New Testament presents the Christian life as much more than regulated behavior. Indeed, to take the New Testament as a law book seriously misconstrues the nature of the Christian gospel—both as to what it proclaims and as to what it calls for by way of response. The problems with such a use of the New Testament for ethical theory and practice boil down to two: (1) such an approach does not create moral beings, but only controls the worst features of non-moral behavior; and (2) laws require an accompanying body of oral or written interpretations to explicate and apply them in new situations. Sadly, history reveals that where an accompanying authoritative tradition comes into play in order to relate Scripture as a set of laws to the contemporary situation, all too often the tradition takes precedence over Scripture—as witness, for example, rabbinic codifications, Roman Catholic ecclesiastical law, and the many Protestant cultic expressions of the Christian faith.

In matters of personal morality where the biblical commands to love and honor are taken seriously, a law-book approach to the New Testament may work out fairly well, particularly when a person internalizes love and honor and develops new attitudes. But a law-book approach apart from some accompanying body of tradition (whether written or oral) seldom has much to say about social ethics, simply because circumstances change so rapidly that codified laws are soon outdated. Jesus, for example, said nothing specific about life in a geriatrics ward, or about collective bargaining, or about genocide. And those who take the New Testament as an ethical law-book find that they too have very little to say as Christians about such matters.

A second way of using the New Testament for ethical guidance is that which places all of the emphasis on the universal principles which can be found to underlie the New Testament accounts. Here the particular statements and practices of the New Testament are not considered binding, but the principles behind them are. It was Adolf Harnack's *What is Christianity?* originally given as a series of non-technical lectures in Berlin during the winter of 1899–1900 under the title "Das Wesen des Christentums," that popularized this approach. For Harnack, the difference between the Jewish law-book approach to religion and Jesus' approach was this:

> They thought of God as a despot guarding the ceremonial ob-servances in his household; he breathed in the presence of God. They saw him only in his law, which they had converted into a labyrinth of dark defiles, blind alleys and secret passages; he saw and felt him everywhere. They were in possession of a thou-sand of his commandments, and thought therefore that they knew him; he had one only, and knew him by it. They had made this religion into an earthly trade, and there was nothing more detestable; he proclaimed the living God and the soul's nobility.[1]

Jesus' message, as Harnack saw it, can be summed up under three headings: (1) the kingdom of God and its coming; (2) God the Father and the infinite value of the human soul; and (3) the higher righteousness and the commandment of love. In the final analysis, however, these three emphases, as Har-nack understood them, coalesced into something of a Christ-inspired religious humanism, for "ultimately the kingdom is nothing but the treasure which the soul possesses in the eter-nal and merciful God. It needs only a few touches to develop this thought into everything that, taking Jesus' sayings as its groundwork, Christendom has known and striven to maintain as hope, faith and love."[2]

Such a focus on the underlying principles of the New Testament—and, in fact, on the Bible as a whole—provides a means for appreciating how biblical norms can be applied to changing situations, both in the areas of personal morality and social morality. For while the Bible reflects various laws suited for different and differing situations, behind those laws are principles which have remained fixed because they are universal in nature. It is therefore the task of the interpreter, so this view maintains, to look beneath the rules and regu-lations having to do with particular problems in order to dis-cern the universal principles which gave rise to such legislation, and, after discovering them, to apply those same principles to the issues of the present day.

---

[1]Harnack, *What is Christianity?* trans. J. R. Wilkinson (London: Wil-liams & Norgate, 1901), pp. 50–51.

[2]Harnack, *What is Christianity?* p. 77.

The problems with such an approach, however, are numerous—though their intensity varies considerably depending on the skill and sensitivity of individual interpreters. Two major problems in particular tend to recur: (1) in the search for universal principles it is all too easy to turn biblical theology into philosophy, with Jesus Christ heard only as an echo of Socrates; and (2) Christian ethics often becomes a subcategory of natural law, with the moral imperative of life rooted in man himself and human reason viewed as the main guide for moral judgments.

A third way of using the New Testament in ethical decision-making is that which places all the stress on God's free and sovereign encounter through his Spirit with a person as he or she reads Scripture, and the ethical direction given for the particular moment in such an encounter. Indeed, Scripture as a record of God's past encounters and the Spirit as the agent of such encounters can never be separated, for God has chosen to meet men and women and to reveal his will to them through the Scriptures. Yet neither the Old nor the New Testament, it is asserted, gives us a descriptive ethic in the form of either laws or principles. What the Christian finds in reading the Scriptures is that there he or she is met by the sovereign God who himself defines the "good" for that particular moment and places on the obedient heart an imperative for action.

Emil Brunner was one of the most illustrious modern advocates of this position, and his *The Divine Imperative* is devoted to laying the theological basis for such a view, and "thinking through the concrete problems of particular spheres of life" in light of this approach. In the chapter called "The Definition of Christian Ethic," Brunner sets forth this position concisely:

> Whatever can be defined in accordance with a principle—whether it be the principle of pleasure or the principle of duty—is legalistic. . . . The Christian moralist and the extreme individualist are at one in their emphatic rejection of legalistic conduct; they join hands, as it were, in face of the whole host of legalistic moralists; they are convinced that conduct which is regulated by abstract principles can never be good. . . . There is no Good save obedient behaviour, save the obedient will. But this obedience is rendered not to a law or a principle which can

be known beforehand, but only to the free, sovereign will of God. The Good consists in always doing what God wills at any particular moment.[3]

Later, in discussing "The Divine Command as Gift and Demand," Brunner insists that "in a Christian ethic we are not dealing with 'counsels' nor with exhortations, nor with 'values'," but rather "we are confronted by a Command which must be taken in dead earnest."[4] It is true, Brunner acknowledges, that the New Testament represents its authors as frequently exhorting their readers. But here he sees a major difference between the Old and the New Testament, for in the Old Testament it is commands, not exhortations, that are given. And he goes on to insist,

> The form of the exhortation is simply intended to remind us of the ground on which the Divine claim is based; that is, that every believer can indeed know the will of God for himself, through his faith in Christ. The apostolic exhortation implies that the believer is no longer a minor, and it sweeps away all legalistic heteronomy. Not even an Apostle can tell you what you ought to do; God Himself is the only One who can tell you this. There is to be no intermediary between ourselves and the Divine will. God wishes to deal with us "personally," not through any medium.[5]

Historically, of course, such an emphasis on God's sovereign encounter and his personal direction of life came like a breath of fresh air amid the often arid formulations and withering regulations of Christian theology, whether liberal or conservative. It seemed to free the Christian for authentic ethical living before God in both the personal and the societal areas of life. Yet many today have backed off from an exclusive acceptance of such a position, believing that in its renunciation of propositional revelation it makes Christian theology too subjective, and in its disavowal of laws and principles it makes Christian ethics too individualistic. Today there is a widespread appreciation of the need for God by his Spirit to encounter individuals through the Scriptures for there to be

[3]Brunner, *The Divine Imperative*, trans. O. Wyon (London: Lutterworth, 1937), pp. 82–83.

[4]Brunner, *The Divine Imperative*, p. 118.

[5]Brunner, *The Divine Imperative*, p. 118.

authentic Christian conversion, authentic Christian theology, and authentic Christian life. But there is also a widespread hesitancy to deny to the Bible any intrinsic authority in favor of only an instrumental authority and to exclude all external criteria as factors in the direction of life.

The fourth way of using the New Testament in ethical decision-making and practice arises largely out of the third approach, and shares with it an opposition to prescriptive laws and principles. It differs, however, from the third in laying primary emphasis on the individual's response to whatever situations are confronted. Several variations of this approach have been proposed, but all of them can be described by the term "contextualism," or "situation ethics." What this view argues is that rather than looking to laws or principles, which is the essence of legalism—or even to an encounter with God as providing the ethical criteria, for that is much too subjective—Christians can determine what should be done in any particular case simply by getting the facts of the situation clearly in view, and then asking themselves, What is the loving thing to do in this case? Such an approach, of course, does not entirely rule out the prescriptive, for it accepts love as the one great principle for life. Yet it insists that "the law of love" allows no predefinition for action in any given circumstance, but must be reapplied separately and moment by moment in every situation faced. Nor are all biblical exhortations set aside by a situation ethic. They are, however, treated as tactical suggestions rather than prescriptive norms—that is, as cautionary advice indicating how matters usually work out, but advice which should be set aside whenever the principle of love in the situation requires it. The major question in every ethical exigency, therefore, is simply this: What single act or set of actions will prove most love-embodying and love-fulfilling in the present situation?

Perhaps the best example of a contextual approach is Paul Lehmann's *Ethics in a Christian Context*, which argues for "a *koinonia* ethic" and defines that ethic as one that *"is concerned with relations and functions, not with principles and precepts."*[6]

---

[6]Lehmann, *Ethics in a Christian Context* (New York: Harper & Row, 1963), p. 124 (italics his).

Joseph Sittler's *The Structure of Christian Ethics* is of the same type, though more flamboyant. In discussing the Sermon on the Mount, for example, Sittler argues for an ethic like that of Jesus which "cracks all rabbinical patterns, transcends every statuary solidification of duty, breaks out of all systematic schematizations of the good—and out of the living, perceptive, restorative passion of faith enfolds in its embrace the fluctuant, incalculable, novel emergents of human life."[7] And this approach was popularized by Joseph Fletcher in his *Situation Ethics: The New Morality*.[8]

Certainly situation ethics has much to say in the area of social morality—though it is often less vocal with regard to personal morality. To do the loving thing in each situation of life is highly laudatory. But while love must always motivate and condition every human action if such actions are to be truly ethical, love as the sole criterion for ethical decision-making is highly suspect. Like the classical utilitarian principles of "the greatest happiness" and "the greatest good," love as a moral criterion is an easily adjustable norm. When set in a theological context, it may carry a fairly standard meaning because of its association with other concepts. When defined within a humanistic or naturalistic framework, however, it signals other sets of ideas and other meanings. During the sixties and early seventies, the ethics of contextualism appeared to many to be eminently Christian. But there has been a decided retreat from situation ethics of late simply because of its refusal to allow any predefinitions for the nature and content of love, and its blithe optimism that individuals, given only encouragement, will usually act lovingly when they understand the various facets, ramifications, and implications of the particular situation—an optimism that utterly disregards human egoism, stupidity, and cruelty, as repeatedly testified to by history and personal experience.

We began this section by speaking of a hermeneutical dilemma set up in the minds of many by four competing models of how to use the New Testament in ethical decision-

---

[7]Sittler, *The Structure of Christian Ethics* (Baton Rouge: Louisiana State University Press, 1958), p. 48.

[8]Fletcher, *Situation Ethics: The New Morality* (Philadelphia: Westminster Press, 1966).

making and practice. Then we laid out, in brief, the substance of these four approaches. It must be said, however, that not everyone who speaks of laws in the Bible is an Orthodox Jew, a Roman Catholic, or a Protestant Fundamentalist. Nor is everyone who stresses ethical principles a classical liberal; nor everyone who speaks of a Christ-encounter an existentialist; nor everyone who gives attention to the particular situation a contextualist. It may be that each of these approaches is more wrong in what it denies than in what it proposes, and that each in its own way is setting forth a necessary aspect of truth for a Christian ethic—some, admittedly, more than others, but each to some degree highlighting an aspect of truth that is minimized or neglected by others. But that can be determined only as we move beyond mere description to evaluation, which we undertake next.

B. SOME BASIC BIBLICAL PERSPECTIVES

Every process of evaluation requires the acceptance of a stance from which to view the data and weigh the evidence. Without such a stance, the rendering of value judgments and the integration of knowledge would be impossible. Various stances, of course, have been and are being advocated for interpreting the data of life, with each requiring both theoretical and experiential testing. As Christians we affirm that the Bible is the touchstone for faith and life, and we believe that it is only on the basis of the perspectives provided by the Bible that we can make adequate sense out of the data of life and be led to think and act aright before God. It is therefore necessary for us to remind ourselves here of some of the basic biblical perspectives in the area of ethics, with the hope that they will shed some light on how to resolve our initial hermeneutical dilemma. Then we will be in a position to propose a way of understanding the various statements and practices of the New Testament that relate to our subject of social morality.

Basic to the ethical teaching of the Bible is the insistence that the final measure for human conduct is not to be derived from individuals but stems from the nature of God, from the quality of his love for mankind, and from the character of his redemptive activity. "Be holy because I, the Lord your God, am holy" (Lev. 19:2; cf. 11:44–45; 20:7; 1 Pet. 1:16) is a typical ethical maxim that spans both testaments. Likewise, the depiction of God's love as expressed in his mighty acts on behalf of his people (cf. Exod. 20:2; Pss. 105, 106), in his personal relations with his people (cf. Isa. 54:5–8; Hos. 1–14; Heb. 12:5–12), and pre-eminently in sending his Son for our redemption (cf. John 3:16; 1 John 4:9–10) is the basis for the injunction, "Dear friends, since God so loved us, we also ought to love one another" (1 John 4:11). Throughout the Bible, in fact, the pattern for social morality among God's people is what God in his great love has done for humankind, and all appeals to an ethical life are based on that. There are no depictions of the merits of particular cases; no analyses of the intrinsic worth of certain actions; no sociological surveys laying out a consensus of opinion that should be followed. Rather, the Bible portrays in bold and gripping terms what God has done for man and urges a response of like quality directed both to God and to one's fellows.

A corollary to this first perspective is a second: that the moral teaching of the Bible is always presented in closest relation to the Bible's message as a whole, which means that ethics for a Christian can never be considered either some autonomous entity or a trivial matter. Atheistic and naturalistic systems of thought view morality as wholly autonomous, independent of divine sanctions and supportable only because of social desirability or some intrinsic value. The mystery religions of the Greek world tended to trivialize ethics in their disparagement of the material world and their stress on salvation as being for the soul alone. The Bible, however, always joins theology and ethics, and always insists that the one cannot exist without the other—which is why the oral tradition of Judaism emphasized Halakah (that is, "how to walk" or "conduct one's life"), and why some of the most profound Christological statements of the New Testament are set in the midst of ethical exhortations (for example, Phil. 2:6–11; 1 Tim. 3:16).

Yet, thirdly, just because they are of the nature of a response to a holy and loving God, biblical ethics reflect a different value system than do those ethical systems which spring only from social needs. Aristotle's virtues of justice, temperance, fortitude, and prudence in his *Ethics* and *Politics*, for example, were qualities valuable for improving social and civic life. They were means to an end to accomplish a thoroughly this-worldly purpose. The New Testament, however, strikes deeper when it speaks of "love, joy, peace, patience, kindness, goodness, faithfulness, gentleness and self-control" (Gal. 5:12–23; cf. Matt. 5:3–10, 21–48)—virtues which relate more to the quality of the person than to the efficiency of what he or she does, and certainly virtues which are not always viewed as practical or necessary for the welfare of society or the state. Some of the ethical tenets of the New Testament, of course, are merely transpositions into another key of virtues that were traditionally esteemed. Modesty as heightened by Jesus into self-denial is an example, as is alms-giving heightened into sacrificial generosity. Others take on a new meaning when set in a Christian context, as does the simple virtue of neighborliness: "Anyone who gives you a cup of water *in my name because you belong to Christ* will certainly not lose his reward" (Mark 9:41; italics mine). Yet should all such virtues reside in a person, one thing more, according to the Bible, is needful: for pride itself—even pride in these virtues—to be abandoned. For, as J. L. Houlden points out, "where God has shown himself generous to the point of the cross, man is called upon to imitate him and to adopt a new scale of values."[9]

A fourth matter to note when considering basic biblical perspectives is that the New Testament proclaims a message of freedom from codes of law—that is, freedom not only from the delusion that status before God can be gained by keeping his laws ("legalism"), but also from the requirement to express relationship with God in prescribed ways ("nomism").[10] The prophets of the Old Covenant had much to say against legalism, but they never attempted to set aside the Mosaic law as the proper vehicle for the expression of Israel's faith. Life lived under Torah characterized the best of Old Testament piety, and it continues to epitomize the nobler expressions of Ju-

[9]Houlden, *Ethics and the New Testament* (New York: Oxford, 1977), p. 18.
[10]Cf. my "The Pedagogical Nature of the Law in Galatians 3:19–4:7," *Journal of the Evangelical Theological Society*, 25 (1982), 53–61.

daism today. The New Testament, however, rather than laying out detailed codes of conduct for various situations, speaks of the Christian life as being a life of responsible freedom "in Christ." "If the Son sets you free," said Jesus, "you will be free indeed" (John 8:36). "Now that faith has come," insisted Paul, "we are no longer under the supervision of the law" (Gal. 3:25). In fact, as Paul wrote later, God "canceled the written code, with its regulations, that was against us and that stood opposed to us; he took it away, nailing it to the cross" (Col. 2:14). Christians, therefore, have ceased to regard their relationship with God in terms of law at all, either as a means of attaining that relationship or as an expression of it. They know God personally in Christ, and therefore agree with Martin Luther that he who tries to mix faith and works either for attaining righteousness or as the necessary expression of righteousness is (paraphrasing one of Aesop's fables) like "the dog who runs along a stream with a piece of meat in his mouth, and, deceived by the reflection of the meat in the water, opens his mouth to snap at it and so loses both the meat and the reflection."[11]

Still, and fifth in our enumeration of biblical perspectives, Christian freedom is not antinomianism. While the New Testament does not lay out any set of rules for the guidance of conduct, it does set before the Christian an ethical task that is presented as obligatory. In the main, this task is presented in terms of following Jesus' example and teachings, which are given to set a standard for conduct pleasing to God, to indicate the direction in which Christian morality should be moving, and to signal the quality of action to be expressed. As a standard, the example and teaching of Jesus "help towards an intelligent and realistic act of 'repentance', because they offer an objective standard of judgment upon our conduct, so that we know precisely where we stand in the sight of God, and are in a position to accept His judgment upon us and thereby partake of His forgiveness."[12] As indicating direction and quality, "they are intended to offer positive moral guidance

---

[11]"The Freedom of the Christian," *Luther's Works*, vol. 31, ed. H. T. Lehmann (St. Louis: Concordia, 1957), 356.

[12]C. H. Dodd, *Gospel and Law* (Cambridge: Cambridge University Press, 1951), p. 64.

for action, to those who have, in the words of the gospels, received the Kingdom of God."[13] Thus Paul speaks expressly of "the law of Christ" in Galatians 6:2, where he says that in bearing one another's burdens his converts are fulfilling "the law of Christ" (*ton nomon tou Christou*), and in 1 Corinthians 9:21, where he refers to himself as not being lawless in his freedom but being "under Christ's law" (*ennomos Christou*; literally, "in-lawed to Christ"). And so the New Testament writers habitually reflect the teachings of Jesus in their ethical exhortations (cf. Rom. 12–14; 1 Thess. 4:1–12; James passim) and appeal to the example of Jesus as the pattern for Christian living (cf. Phil. 2:5–11; 1 Pet. 4:1).

Two further matters, however, need to be highlighted here, lest Christian ethics be thought of as only a discipline of following Jesus' example and teachings. The first of these (and sixth in our listing of biblical perspectives) is that which Paul puts to the fore in discussing the issues at Corinth and that which distinguishes Christian ethics from all forms of legalism and Stoicism: immediate and personal direction by God through his Holy Spirit (cf. 1 Cor. 2:10–16). Paul identifies this feature of Christian living as "the mind of Christ" (*nous Christou*), meaning by that that Christ's example and teachings become operative in the lives of Christians by means of the activity of the Holy Spirit. Throughout the New Testament the Christian life is presented as being dependent for both its inauguration and its continuance on God's Spirit, who in his ministry confronts men and women with the living Christ, brings them into personal fellowship with God through Christ, and sustains them in all aspects of their new life in Christ. Thus Christians are said to live their lives "in the new way of the Spirit, and not in the old way of the written code" (Rom. 7:6), and Christian ministry is portrayed as being "not of the letter but of the Spirit" (2 Cor. 3:6). This is the realization that caused Paul to speak of the Christian as a "spiritual man" (1 Cor. 2:15; 3:1) and of the Christian life as a "fellowship with the Spirit" (Phil. 2:1) as well as a "fellowship with his Son Jesus Christ" (1 Cor. 1:9).

Finally, it is necessary to remind ourselves that ethics in

---

[13]Dodd, *Gospel and Law*, p. 64.

the Bible are always set in relational contexts. Israel had been brought into covenant relationship with God, and Jewish life was to be lived in response to that relationship and with the interests of the community always in view. Christians have also been brought into covenant relationship with God through Christ, and our lives are likewise to be lived in response to that relationship and with the interests of the corporate Body of Christ always in view. So morality according to the Bible is not something either received in isolation or expressed in isolation. Rather, it is that which proclaims by its every endeavor an existing relationship with God and which works itself out always with the particular circumstances of people in view. In that sense, therefore, biblical ethics may legitimately be called contextual or situational ethics—though perhaps, as some would insist, only after considerable disinfecting and rebaptizing of those terms for more appropriate use.

C. TOWARD A RESOLUTION OF THE DILEMMA

Do these perspectives shed any light on our hermeneutical dilemma of how the New Testament should be used in moral decision-making and practice? Some may feel compelled to answer such a question differently. But if the seven biblical perspectives listed above have been expressed anywhere near correctly, both as to substance and as to emphasis, I believe that they shed a great deal of light on our question and go far to resolving our dilemma.

On the basis of these seven points, we must say, in the first place, that the ethical statements of the New Testament are to be taken with prescriptive and obligatory force, and not just as tactical suggestions which may or may not be heeded by Christians. That is the truth of the position which takes the New Testament as a book of laws for ethical conduct—though to express this truth in the way in which that first position does seriously distorts the true nature of Christian morality. Second, the ethical statements of the New Testament are given not as detailed codes of conduct but as principles or precepts which seek primarily to set a standard for the kind of life pleasing to God, to indicate the direction in which we ought to be moving, and to signal the quality of life our actions ought to be expressing. That is the truth of the position which wants to abstract universal principles from the various ethical statements and actions of the New Testament—though, again, to state this truth in a way which turns theology into philosophy and special revelation into natural law seriously distorts Christian morality.

Third, for there to be an ethic that in any sense can be called Christian, there must be the direct action of the Holy Spirit in the Christian's life and in the particular circumstances confronted. Indeed, not only does the Spirit regenerate; he also gives guidance as to how the principles of Christ should be applied in given situations and empowers the Christian to put these directives into effect. That is the truth of the position which places all of the emphasis on God's direct encounter with a person through his Spirit. And, fourth, for any action to be truly Christian, it must be expressive of a relationship with God through Christ and must work itself out with attention to the specific situations it encounters, always motivated and conditioned by love for God and love for one's fellows. That is the element of truth in any contextual system of ethics.

How, then, should we resolve our hermeneutical dilemma regarding the use of the New Testament in ethical theory and practice? Without attempting to be too eclectic, yet recognizing elements of truth in each of the four proposed models on the basis of the biblical perspectives enumerated above, we should probably define New Testament ethics as follows: prescriptive principles stemming from the heart of the gospel (usually embodied in the example and teachings of Jesus), which are meant to be applied to specific situations by the direction and enablement of the Holy Spirit, being always motivated and conditioned by love. Such a definition is important to provide a hermeneutical beginning. To go further requires a methodology, which I would like to propose in the next chapter.

II. A DEVELOPMENTAL HERMENEUTIC:
New Treasures as well as Old

At the conclusion of his parables of the kingdom, Matthew's Gospel portrays Jesus as asking his disciples, "Have you understood all these things?" (13:51). When they answered "Yes," he gave them another parable: "Every teacher of the law who has been instructed about the kingdom of heaven is like the owner of a house who brings out of his storeroom new treasures as well as old" (13:52).

Many features of this brief, concluding parable are fairly easy to understand. The "kingdom of heaven" is certainly the reign of God in the life as proclaimed by, effected by, and focused in Jesus, for the use of "kingdom" in Matthew is Christocentrically oriented throughout. Likewise, "the teacher of the law who has been instructed about the kingdom" is one who is committed to and instructed by Jesus—that is, a Christian teacher,[1] not some Jewish scribe trained in Pharisaic traditions. It is also obvious that the parable has something to do with how Christians are to interpret divine revelation and apply its message to their day, for it comes at the end of

[1]The use of *mathēteutheis* ("who has been discipled/trained/instructed") in 13:52a has often been seen as a pun on the name Matthew (*Matthaios*), and so a veiled reference to the evangelist himself or a "school" which honored his name. Benno Przybylski, however, has shown that the broad use of "disciple" in Matthew's Gospel refers to "people in general who have accepted (13:52, 27:57) or will accept (28:19) the teaching of Jesus"—i.e., Christians generally, not just a circle of learned men within the evangelist's community (*Righteousness in Matthew and His World of Thought* [Cambridge: Cambridge University Press, 1980], pp. 109–10). Cf. also J. D. Kingsbury, *The Parables of Jesus in Matthew 13: A Study in Redaction-Criticism* (London: S. P. C. K., 1969), pp. 126–29.

a group of seven parables which do just that for the disciples. Furthermore, the parable suggests that in interpretation it is Jesus' pattern which is to be in some manner the paradigm for Christian teachers—that is, just as Jesus' pattern of ministry is to be the paradigm for Christian discipleship ("It is enough for the student to be like his teacher, and the servant like his master"; Matt. 10:25), so Jesus' manner of interpretation is to have some bearing on how Christians interpret and apply Scripture. Thus, as Jesus is portrayed in Matthew's Gospel as a new and better Moses (especially in chapters 5–7), so here his disciples are exhorted to be new and better scribes of the kingdom.

The most difficult feature in the parable, however, is Jesus' comparison of Christian teachers to a householder "who brings out of his storeroom new treasures as well as old." What did Jesus mean by "new" and what by "old"? As Christians today who seek to interpret and proclaim the Christian message, what are we to understand by the phrase "new treasures as well as old" and how are we to relate the new and the old?

Most commentators have concluded that what is meant here by "old" and "new" is what we would call the religion of Israel and the message of the New Testament—that is, "the Old Dispensation of Judaism," "the Mosaic law," and/or "the Old Testament promises," on the one hand, and on the other, "the New Dispensation which has come with Christ," "the fulfilment of the Mosaic law in Jesus' ministry," and/or "Jesus' own teaching."[2] Some understand "old" and "new" to refer more broadly to some such concepts as "the Holy Scriptures and the disciples' own inward experience of what true religion is" or "the Old Evangel of the Bible and the new insights of recent scholarship." And a few have despaired of ever being

[2]E.g., A. W. Argyle: "The ideal disciple is a rabbi with understanding of the Kingdom, who can therefore bring forth from a well-stored mind *the old*, i.e., the riches of Old Testament truth, and *the new*, i.e., the riches of the new teaching of Jesus" (*The Gospel according to Matthew* [Cambridge: Cambridge University Press, 1963], p. 108); David Hill: "*What is new and what is old*: these phrases probably connote either traditional Jewish teaching on the Kingdom of God which had now been renewed completely by the presence of Jesus, or the ancient OT promises which had found fulfilment in Jesus' person and teaching" (*The Gospel of Matthew* [London: Marshall, Morgan & Scott, 1972], p. 240). Cf. also the commentaries by T. H. Robinson, R. V. G. Tasker, F. V. Filson, W. F. Albright, et al.

able to determine what the words might have meant, either to Jesus or to Matthew.[3]

Recently, however, there has been a tendency to view the old and new of Matthew 13:52 in terms of the gospel proclamation which has as its focus the teaching and ministry of Jesus, and fuller understandings and new applications of that proclamation for various new circumstances faced by Christian prophets and teachers—including, of course, Matthew's own shaping of the Jesus tradition in his Gospel for his own community and audience.[4] And with this I agree. So I argue that here Jesus speaks of the Christian teacher as one who is rooted in the gospel proclamation (its foundation in the salvation history of the Old Testament, its message of redemption in Christ Jesus, its derived principles, and its described practices), and one who is relevant to current times and circumstances by understanding more fully and applying more adequately that proclamation to his or her own situation.

A. THE CONJUNCTION OF OLD AND NEW IN THE BIBLICAL RECORDS

Throughout the Bible there is the conjunction of the old and the new. God's revelation of his will in the Old Testament was given progressively in Israel's history, being related to

---

[3]E.g., B. T. D. Smith: "It is impossible to determine the original meaning of the words" (*S. Matthew*, in the *Cambridge Greek Testament*, ed. A. Nairne [Cambridge: Cambridge University Press, 1950], p. 141). F. C. Grant wrote, "This precious saying described the Christian teacher," but preferred to say nothing as to what it might mean (in *Nelson's Bible Commentary*, VI [New York: Thomas Nelson, 1962], 78).

[4]E.g., E. Schweizer: "The true teacher of the Law has learned from Jesus to see both the old and the new together (cf. Wisd. 8:8)—God's Law, and its new interpretation proclaimed by Jesus and realized in all that he does. Or is Matthew thinking of Jesus' own teaching, and its new interpretation in the 'learned' decisions of the community of disciples (16:19; 18:18)?" (*The Good News according to Matthew*, trans. D. E. Green [Atlanta: John Knox, 1975], p. 315); F. W. Beare: "The 'old' and the 'new' could mean the ancient Law of Israel, written and oral, on the one hand; and the interpretation and application given to it by Jesus, on the other. But we are tempted to feel that for the evangelist it means the tradition of the teaching given by Jesus and the interpretation and application which is now supplied by the evangelist" (*The Gospel According to Matthew* [San Francisco: Harper & Row, 1981], p. 317).

his personal relations with his people (e.g., through the covenants) and his redemptive activity on their behalf (e.g., in the Exodus). And this progressive revelation—though important and applicable for that day—pointed forward toward future, fuller revelations of God, which would culminate in the coming of God's Anointed One, the Messiah (cf., e.g., Gen. 3:15; Deut. 18:15, 18; Jer. 31:31–34; Mal. 3:1). So in the Old Testament the Latter Prophets reinterpret the Former Prophets and the Writings make new applications of the words of the Law—not opposing the former, but expressing their significance more fully and applying their message to new situations. Perhaps the most obvious examples of this conjunction of old and new in the Old Testament are in Daniel 9, where Jeremiah's prophecy of seventy years (cf. Jer. 24:12ff.) is reinterpreted to mean "seventy heptads" and to have eschatological significance beyond what was initially thought (cf. esp. vv. 1–3, 20–27), and in Psalm 110, where the Canaanite chieftain Melchizedek of Genesis 14 is brought into the lineage of Israel as one of the nation's ancient worthies (cf. v. 4).

More particularly, in the New Testament there is a similar conjunction of old and new. The earliest preaching of the apostles, we are told, was cast almost entirely in personal terms and functional categories:

> "Jesus of Nazareth was a man accredited by God to you by miracles, wonders and signs, which God did among you through him, as you yourselves know. This man was handed over to you by God's set purpose and foreknowledge; and you, with the help of wicked men, put him to death by nailing him to the cross. But God raised him from the dead, freeing him from the agony of death, because it was impossible for death to keep its hold on him." (Acts 2:22–24)

It was a message that stressed God's intervention in human affairs in Jesus of Nazareth and focused on God's redemption of mankind through what Jesus as Messiah did. Presupposed in that message, of course, were many theological nuances. But full-blown theological formulations and developed ethical stances were, at first, largely held in the substratum of the apostles' early preaching and appear only in the overtones of their message.

As Jews, the apostles and early Christians possessed a basic theology regarding God's person and divine redemption. As Christians, however, their distinctive theological affirmations and their ethical exhortations were derived from God's self-revelation and redemptive activity in Jesus. They worked in their thinking from functional categories (i.e., what God did in and through Jesus) to theological, ontological, and speculative categories (i.e., how this should be understood; who Jesus is; why it all came about; and what it means for everyday living). So in the New Testament we have a record of how these early Christians began to work out the nuances of their basically functional "New Covenant" stance—under, we believe, the guidance of God's Spirit—into a rudimentary system of Christian doctrine and a rudimentary style of Christian living. Thus the New Testament, paralleling the Old Testament in this regard, contains both the record of God's progressive revelation of himself and of his unfolding redemption on behalf of mankind, and accounts of his people's developing endeavors to work out the theological ramifications and ethical implications of that revelation and redemption.

Jesus' promise of the Spirit as recorded in John 14–16 includes the expectation that there would be fuller understandings of his teachings and ministry on the part of his disciples in the future—fuller understandings not divorced from Jesus but rooted in all that Jesus said and did:

> "I have much more to say to you, more than you can now bear. But when he, the Spirit of truth, comes, he will guide you into all truth. He will not speak on his own; he will speak only what he hears, and he will tell you what is yet to come." (16:12–13)

In two places in John's Gospel there are references to biblical interpretation as being more perceptive after Jesus' ascension, and suggestions that the ministry of the Spirit was understood by the earliest Christians to include advances in the understanding of Scripture. In John 2 we are told that it was only after Jesus' resurrection that his disciples understood Psalm 69:9 in the context of Jesus' ministry: "His disciples remembered that it is written: 'Zeal for your house will consume me.' . . . After he was raised from the dead, his disciples recalled what he had said. Then they believed the Scripture and the words that Jesus had spoken" (2:17, 22). And in John 12, of Jesus' entry into Jerusalem and the use of Psalm 118:25–26 and Zechariah 9:9 in that connection, we are told: "At first his disciples did not understand all this. Only after Jesus was glorified did they realize that these things had been written about him and that they had done these things to him" (12:16). In these two accounts—one at the beginning of the evangelist's "Book of Signs" and the other at its close—the disciples are presented as coming to understand certain actions and sayings of Jesus in light of the Old Testament only at a later time—along, of course, the general lines of interpretation laid out by Jesus, but without any direct word from him.

In fact, each of the four Gospels in its own way evidences how the canonical evangelists attempted to be both true to the proclamation which they received and relevant to the particular situations which they faced. Each is a recasting of the original gospel tradition to meet specific issues and concerns within their respective communities addressed, as the application of redaction criticism so abundantly illustrates. Likewise, Paul's letters evidence this wedding of old and new in their pastoral applications of the gospel to various theological and ethical problems in the churches. One particularly obvious conjunction of what Jesus was known to have taught and Paul's application of the thrust of that teaching for a somewhat different situation can be found in 1 Corinthians 7. For in verses 10–11 Paul quotes a saying of Jesus as settling one matter—"To the married I give this command (not I, but the Lord)"—while in verses 12ff., with regard to a further matter on which the church possessed no explicit word of Jesus, he speaks as one authoritatively expressing the gospel's intent: "To the rest I say this (I, not the Lord)." But this is only one fairly obvious example. In the following chapters much more will be said to demonstrate this point for both Paul and the Gospel writers.

B. CHRISTIAN THEOLOGY AS A STORY OF DEVELOPMENT

The history of Christian theology is a story of development. In the Bible we have the record of God's progressive revelation and unfolding redemption in Israel's history, in (pre-eminently) Jesus' ministry, and in the apostolic Church's witness; and accounts of his people's developing endeavors to work out the theological ramifications and ethical implications of that revelation and redemption. But neither the Bible as a whole nor the New Testament in particular gives us the final word on the formulation of Christian theology—at least, not final in the sense that nothing more can or need be said. Rather, the New Testament (building on the Jewish Scriptures) is the touchstone for Christian theology in that it presents the proclamation of God's definitive word to humankind in the person and ministry of Jesus of Nazareth, and the paradigm of how the implications involved in God's revelatory and redemptive activity were begun to be spelled out in the apostolic period. To learn the full story of Christian theology to date, one must also be a student of church history, for under the guidance of the same Spirit who inspired the biblical writings there has been a progressive illumination throughout the past nineteen centuries of the meaning and significance of God's definitive activity in Christ Jesus. To be a Christian theologian today, therefore, requires (1) extensive familiarity with the Scriptures, (2) extensive familiarity with church history, (3) discernment in appreciating the essence and direction of the biblical statements, (4) discernment in distinguishing between advances and pitfalls in the history of Christian thought, being able to identify the lines of continuity which exist between every true advance and the New Testament, the touchstone for Christian faith, and (5) creative ability to say what all this means for Christian faith and life today amid the complexities of varying ideologies and competing lifestyles.

The New Testament, therefore, is not a textbook on systematic theology. It is a record of God's revelation and redemption in Jesus Christ and a record of the Church's initial attempts to understand and state what all that means. To be biblical is not to say only what the New Testament says, "nothing more or less," as some would claim. Rather, the biblical Christian realizes that the Bible, history, and reason all come into play in constructing a Christian theology: the first as the touchstone for truth and as the pointer to the path that should be followed; the second as a record of how the Church has tread that path throughout the centuries, with attention to both the advances and the pitfalls; the third in determining where the history of theology has been in continuity with its revelational base and how Christian theology should be expressed today.

Admittedly, the concept of development in theology is a relatively modern one. Jewish interpreters saw their work in terms of conservation, distillation, and application, but not as a creative enterprise or an objective advance of content. Jesus ben Sirach, for example, the author of the early second-century Wisdom writing we call Sirach (or Ecclesiasticus, "The Church's Book," as Jerome called it), thought of himself as "one that gleans after the grape-gatherers" (i.e., the Sages) and whose work was to distill for posterity the essence of the Sages' wisdom (cf. Sirach 33:16–18). So, too, the Pharisees, the Apocalypticists, the Dead Sea Covenanters, the Tannaitic and Amoraitic Rabbis of the Talmud, the Gaonim, and the Rishonim (e.g., Rashi and Maimonides)—to name only a few prominent schools of Jewish interpretation—saw their tasks mainly (if not exclusively) in terms of conservation, distillation, and application. Likewise, the Church Fathers, the medieval exegetes, and even the Reformers (Luther, Calvin, et al.) saw their treatments of Scripture not as developments but as summaries (compendia) and distillations. They might have looked on their writings as being creative in the sense of an increasing subjective understanding and contemporary applications. But they would not have considered them developments in the content of Christian theology, nor did they have any awareness of developments within Scripture. Yet virtually all modern historians of theology agree that, despite their claims to the contrary, almost all of the Jewish and Christian interpreters mentioned above have, in fact, produced writings that go beyond mere compendia with contemporary applications. In a real sense, each in his own way has been creative and has treated Scripture in a manner that has affected theology objectively.

It was in the nineteenth century that the concept of development assumed prominence in theology. People were conscious of significant achievements in science, technology, exploration, trade, and the arts, and so began to view all human endeavor in terms of progress both quantitatively and qualitatively.[5] More significantly for our purposes, a number of works were written during the nineteenth century by eminent theologians representing all shades of the theological spectrum advocating a developmental understanding of the progress of Christian doctrine since the close of the New Testament canon—with some also arguing for a development of doctrine within the canon. John Henry Newman's *An Essay on the Development of Christian Doctrine* (1845), of course, was seminal. But just as important were Auguste Sabatier's *The Apostle Paul: A Sketch of the Development of His Doctrine* (1870; ET, 1896), Robert Rainy's *The Delivery and Development of Christian Doctrine* (1874), Adolf Harnack's *History of Dogma* (1886; ET, 1905), and James Orr's *The Progress of Dogma* (1901). Likewise, today the concept of development is very much at the fore, both in Protestant and Catholic circles and among both evangelical and liberal scholars.

Yet while almost everyone today is prepared to speak of the development of Christian doctrine over the past two millennia, and while many would also speak of development within the Scriptures themselves (whether under the rubric of "progressive revelation" or the more mundane "evolution of religion"), three quite different models of development have been proposed.[6] First, there are those who take the relationship of later formulations to earlier foundations to be essentially one of identity or sameness, with what appear to be later innovations only more precise explications and applications of what was already implicit earlier. The analogy to be drawn is that of a syllogism, where what appears to be an innovation in the conclusion is only the logical deduction drawn from the major and minor premises and is new only in the sense that it had not been seen to be the case before. This was the attitude of the Alexandrian Fathers (e.g., Clem-

---

[5]For a helpful treatment of the history of doctrinal development, see Peter Toon's *The Development of Doctrine in the Church* (Grand Rapids, Mich.: Eerdmans, 1979).

[6]On these three models, see M. F. Wiles, *The Remaking of Christian Doctrine* (London: SCM, 1974), pp. 4–9.

ent of Alexandria, Origen),[7] and it continues to be the view of development taken in many Catholic, Reformed, and Puritan circles that are more traditionally oriented.

A second model proposed for understanding development is one that speaks of both continuity with a foundational core and genuine growth in conceptualization and expression. It is a model that appeals by way of analogy to the relationship between a growing plant and its original seed, and which argues that real growth always involves genuine innovations of structure (e.g., the stalk, leaves, and flower of a plant are not just reproductions of the original seed), yet that growth is always controlled and judged by what is inherent in the seed itself. It is a model which speaks of "organic growth" (as did Newman, Rainy, and Orr), which encourages us to look for germinal expressions incorporating within themselves indications of a proper course of development and by which we may test all succeeding developments, and which calls on us to attempt to trace out the various and often varying stages of growth as they appear at different times and under diverse circumstances thereafter. This was the approach of the Antiochian Fathers (e.g., Chrysostom, Theodore),[8] and it has come to characterize the methodology of the more constructive and moderate theologians of our day, whatever their particular confessional stance.

A third way of understanding development is that which emphasizes the innovations in the growth of doctrine and minimizes any necessary propositional connection with the foundational core. It stresses environmental and ideological changes in history that have brought about innovative, even contradictory, reformulations of Christian thought. And it justifies its use of the adjective "Christian" in these reformulations not on the basis of any propositional correspondence to earlier doctrines but on the similarity of religious aim and faith. This is the model of an existentialist writing of Christian theology with its insistence on the historically unconnected

---

[7]On an "Alexandrian" approach to Paul among the Ante-Nicene Fathers, see M. F. Wiles, *The Divine Apostle: The Interpretation of St. Paul's Epistles in the Early Church* (Cambridge: Cambridge University Press, 1967), passim.

[8]On an "Antiochian" approach, see Wiles' *The Divine Apostle*, passim.

and momentary nature of God's encounter with humankind. It has come to expression most vocally in New Testament circles in the writings of Rudolf Bultmann and his many disciples.[9]

While, admittedly, scholars differ on what is meant by "the development of Christian doctrine," almost all speak of the history of Christian thought as a story of development. Our own view is in line with an "organic" understanding (the second model above), using the analogy of an original seed to the stalk, leaves, and flower of a plant. Better yet, the analogy could be of a young man fervently in love with a young woman, whose love may have numerous psychological and physiological presuppositions unrecognized by him and whose early love-letters may fail to express all that his heart and mind feel, but who, as he grows in understanding and draws on the stock of ideas available to him in his culture, comes over a period of time to be able to understand more adequately and to express more fully his love, together with its ramifications and implications. This is not to imply that theological development is always a continuous and culminative growth in only one direction. Seed sometimes grows in spurts and in aberrant ways, and so, sadly, does love. So in theology, as in all of life, there is the need to develop healthy growth patterns, to be able to identify continuity as well as development, and to be conservative in our reaching back to our revelational base as well as creative in our moving forward to a fuller understanding and a better application. Thus, as there is the conjunction of old and new in the Bible, so there has been the conjunction of old and new throughout the history of Christian thought. And it is this realization that we must keep in mind in seeking to understand the relation of New Testament theology generally and New Testament social ethics in particular to our day.

C. A PROPOSED UNDERSTANDING OF NEW TESTAMENT ETHICS

Just as the New Testament is no textbook on theology, so it is no compendium of ethical theory and practice. Rather, in

[9]It is found also in Wiles' "non-incarnational" approach to theology in his *The Remaking of Christian Doctrine.*

the area of ethics, what we have in the New Testament is a *declaration* of the gospel and the ethical principles that derive from the gospel, and a *description* of how that proclamation and its principles were put into practice in various situations during the apostolic period. Its proclamation and principles, I argue, are to be taken as normative. The way that proclamation and its principles were put into practice in the first century, however, should be understood as signposts at the beginning of a journey which point out the path to be followed if we are to reapply that same gospel in our day. It will not do simply to ask, Does the New Testament say anything explicit concerning this or that social issue? with the intent being to repeat that answer if it does and to remain silent if its doesn't. Such an approach assumes the record to be a static codification of ethical maxims. Rather, what we need to do is to ask, What principles derived from the gospel proclamation does the New Testament declare to be important for the area of social morality? and What practices in application of these principles does the New Testament describe as setting a paradigm for our reapplication of those same principles today? In answering such questions, we need to be both as expert as possible in historical-cultural-grammatical exegesis and as open as possible to the Spirit's guidance so as to be able to distinguish between declared principles and described practices.

The Church of the first century and the writers of the New Testament did not settle every ethical issue in advance, simply because they were not omniscient and could not see every situation in advance. Nor did God by his Spirit so illuminate them that they could. What they did do, however, was highly significant, both for Christian faith and for Christian living: they proclaimed the message of new life in Christ and they began to work out the implications of that gospel for the situations they encountered—not always, admittedly, as fully or as adequately as we might wish from our later perspectives, but appropriately for their day and pointing the way to a fuller understanding and more adequate application in later times. We should not try to make them out to be all-knowing and all-wise in every area of social concern—or, conversely, disparage them because they weren't. Instead, I suggest, we ought as Christians (1) to attempt to recapture the principles of the gospel in their declarations that have ramifications for social morality, and (2) to endeavor to follow the path that they marked out for the application of those gospel principles, seeking to carry out their work in fuller and more significant ways. In the remaining chapters it will be my task to spell out and illustrate this proposal in three major areas of social concern.

III. THE CULTURAL MANDATE:
Neither Jew nor Greek

In the previous chapter I proposed that what we have in the New Testament with respect to social ethics is a declaration of the gospel and the ethical principles that derive from the gospel, and a description of how those principles were applied in various situations during the apostolic period. The proclamation and its principles, I suggested, come with prescriptive force and serve as the touchstone for all Christian ethical theory and practice. The recorded practices, however, are meant to show how those principles were applied in that day and to point the direction in which we as Christians should be moving in reapplying those same norms in fuller and more significant ways in our day. In this chapter we will consider the cultural mandate of the gospel, dealing with principles inherent in the Christian gospel as proclaimed in the New Testament and the practice of Christians as portrayed in both the New Testament and the annals of church history. At the conclusion I would like to highlight certain implications for Christian social ethics today.

A. CULTURAL DIVISIONS IN THE ANCIENT WORLD

The world in which the message of Christ was first proclaimed was a culturally divided world. Indeed, Alexander the Great had brought all the lands from Greece and Egypt in the west to India in the east within one empire, and had imposed on the people a common language and the veneer of a common culture; and Rome had built on this foundation to establish its laws and political organization from Britain to Mesopotamia. But underlying the surface features of a common empire, common official languages (Greek in the east and Latin in the west), common laws, and the breaking down of travel barriers, there were deep cultural divisions within the first-century world which neither imposed languages nor imposed laws could heal.

Antioch of Syria, for example, the third-largest city of the Roman Empire (after Rome and Alexandria), was noted for its openness, sophistication, and tolerance. It became something of a melting pot of western and eastern cultures, having among its more than 500,000 inhabitants Greeks, Romans, Egyptians, Jews, Arabs, and Persians. Yet even in so noble a city as Antioch, people lived in an atmosphere of cultural tension and racial animosity—as witness the persecutions which broke out against the city's Jews, who made up about one-seventh of the population, during the reign of Caligula (A.D. 37–41) and during the tumultuous middle and late sixties of the first century A.D. And what was true at Antioch was also the case, to varying degrees, throughout the Roman Empire. Peoples were pitted against peoples, classes against classes, religious creeds against religious creeds, philosophical stances against philosophical stances—yet all (supposedly) existed within a common culture and common laws.[1] Sadly, the situation today is much the same.

B. THE MANDATE OF THE GOSPEL

The most forthright statement on social ethics in all the New Testament is found in Galatians 3:28: "There is neither Jew nor Greek, slave nor free, male nor female, for you are all one in Christ Jesus." The statement has been widely heralded as the "Magna Carta of the New Humanity," for it sets forth a relationship "in Christ Jesus" in which believers through baptism not only have been "united with Christ" and "clothed with Christ" (v. 27) but also have entered into a new relationship of oneness with one another. As an indicative state-

---

[1]For an informed, perceptive, and interesting treatment of cultures during the first Christian century, see Edwin Yamauchi's *Harper's World of the New Testament* (San Francisco: Harper & Row, 1981).

ment, it declares that this oneness is already a reality in the sight of God; that, as Otto Michel says, "in the act of baptism all distinctions between men of the old aeon with respect to nationality, salvation history, or social status have been done away."[2] And the passage clearly suggests that on the basis of this new and objective reality a whole new set of attitudes and reactions are to be ours as Christians as we seek to express this reality in the Church and in society.

There has been a good deal of discussion lately regarding early Christian catechetical, confessional, and/or liturgical formulae in the New Testament. And since Heinrich Schlier published his commentary on Galatians in 1949, many have seen verse 28 as part of one of those early confessional portions.[3] Admittedly, the extent of the formula and the exact nature of its components continue to be matters of debate among scholars. I would argue, however, that both the structure and the content of Galatians 3:27–28 indicate that in these two verses we have a liturgical formulation of the early Church which Paul used to support his argument in verses 1–26 and to introduce his conclusion in verse 29. Structurally, one can go from verse 26 to verse 29, omitting verses 27–28, without noticing any break in Paul's logic or grammar. Furthermore, the last clause of verse 28 clearly parallels verse 26 (with the exception of the distinctly Pauline phrase "through faith," *dia tēs pisteōs*, of verse 26), which suggests that the "for" (*gar*) of verse 27 introduces a statement in support of the affirmation of verse 26, and that "as many of you as" (*hosoi*) of verse 27 is meant to clarify and be synonymous with "all" (*pantes*) of verse 26. As for content, it need be noted that only the first pair of coordinates in verse 28 ("neither Jew nor Greek") is directly relevant to Paul's argument in Galatians. Later in the letter, of course, he speaks of slavery and freedom. But his argument there in chapters 4 and 5 concerns spiritual freedom as opposed to spiritual slavery, whereas here, "neither . . . slave nor free" concerns social status; and his words there depend on the reality of the distinction, whereas here they proclaim its abolition. Likewise, Paul has not dealt at all with the relation of the sexes in arguing against the Judaizers at Galatia. Yet here we have the statement that "in Christ Jesus" there is "neither . . . male nor female."

These same pairings are to be found in either abbreviated or expanded form and in the same order at other places in the Pauline letters—which suggests a degree of fixity for the pattern, at least in Paul's mind. First Corinthians 12:13 reads: "For we were all baptized by one Spirit into one body— whether Jews or Greeks, slave or free—and we were all given the one Spirit to drink." Colossians 3:11 says that in the Christian life "there is no Greek or Jew, circumcised or uncircumcised, barbarian, Scythian, slave or free, but Christ is all, and is in all." Likewise, the exhortations of 1 Corinthians 7:17–28 as to being circumcised or uncircumcised (vv. 17–19) and slave or free (vv. 21–23) and concerning marriage (vv. 25–28) are structured in the same order. Furthermore, it should be observed that the pairings of Galatians 3:28 and 1 Corinthians 12:13 appear explicitly in conjunction with the mention of baptism, and those of Colossians 3:11 are inferentially associated as well (cf. 2:12; 3:9–10), yet baptism as such is not being discussed in any of these contexts. This suggests that these pairings were originally formulated in a baptismal liturgy of the early Church.

There is much to be said, therefore, for the view that Galatians 3:28 was originally part of a baptismal confession of early Christians and that Paul has used it in support of his argument in verses 1–29. As Hans Dieter Betz, after a review of such evidence as cited above, concludes:

> One may therefore venture the suggestion that Paul has lifted Gal 3:26–28, in part or as a whole, from a pre-Pauline liturgical context. In the liturgy, the saying would communicate information to the newly initiated, telling them of their eschatological status before God in anticipation of the Last Judgment and also informing them how this status affects, in fact changes their social, cultural, and religious self-understanding, as well as their responsibilities in the here-and-now.
>
> Therefore, Paul's use of the saying in his letter is secondary in function. In the context of the present argument it serves as a 'reminder' and as the cardinal proof. Again, Paul can activate the Galatians' situation of eye-witnesses: they themselves know the things of which Paul is reminding them; they have heard them before and have agreed to them in the decisive ceremony

which had made them members of the Christian church.[4]

Whether or not we agree with Betz that verse 26 should be included within the formula, or hold that it starts at verse 27 (as I view it), the extremely important point to note here is that on the basis of a form-critical analysis the statement of verse 28 cannot be seen as merely some idiosyncratic notion of Paul's but probably should be taken as a confession of first-century Christians more generally—a confession included within the baptismal liturgy of the early Church which proclaims both a new status in Christ before God spiritually and new relationships between believers socially.

Just why these three matters, and not others, were incorporated into the confession of early Christians is impossible to say. Perhaps their inclusion was a conscious attempt to stand in opposition to the three *berakoth* ("blessings," "benedictions") which appear at the beginning of the Jewish cycle of morning prayers: "Blessed be He [God] that He did not make me a Gentile; blessed be He that He did not make me a boor [i.e., an ignorant peasant or a slave]; blessed be He that He did not make me a woman" (credited to R. Judah b. Elai, c. A.D. 150, in Tos Berakoth 7:18 and Jer Berakoth 13b; to R. Meier, his contemporary, in Bab Menahoth 43b).[5] Analogous expressions of "gratitude" appear in Greek writings as well; for example, "that I was born a human being and not a beast, next, a man and not a woman, thirdly, a Greek and not a barbarian" (attributed to Thales and Socrates in Diogenes Laertius' *Vitae Philosophorum* 1.33; to Plato in Plutarch's *Marius* 46.1 and Lactantius' *Divine Institutes* 3.19.17). So it may be surmised that in conscious contrast to such Jewish and Greek chauvinistic statements, early Christians saw it as particularly appropriate to give praise in their baptismal confession that through Christ the old racial schisms and cultural divisions had been healed.

Regardless of how the specific details concerning the provenance of the confession are to be settled, the point to note here is that when first-century Christians spoke of being

[4]Betz, *Galatians* (Philadelphia: Fortress Press, 1979), pp. 184–85.

[5]Cf. *The Authorised Daily Prayer Book of the United Hebrew Congregations of the British Commonwealth of Nations*, trans. S. Singer, 2nd rev. ed. (London: Eyre and Spottiswoode, 1962), pp. 6–7.

"sons of God," "baptized into Christ," and "clothed with Christ" (3:26–27), they also spoke of their faith in terms of a new relationship socially in which there is "neither Jew nor Greek, slave nor free, male nor female" (3:28)—three pairings which cover in embryonic fashion all the essential relationships of humanity. And though the confession appears explicitly only in Paul's letters, it is implicit in the gospel proclamation that resounds throughout the New Testament.

We may, therefore, affirm that inherent in the proclamation of the early Christians was a distinctive cultural mandate: that Jews and Gentiles are to be accepted as having equal standing before God spiritually and within the Church socially when "in Christ." In the redemption provided through Christ, God has eliminated the divisions and inequalities between Jews and Gentiles. Without obliterating racial characteristics, he has provided one way of access for all people unto himself through faith in Jesus Christ. So in his letter to Christians at Rome, while acknowledging Israel's many advantages historically (cf. 3:1–4; 9:4–5), Paul proclaims a gospel of "no difference" (*ou estin diastolē*) between Jews and Gentiles, either in condemnation before God (1:18–3:20) or in access to God by faith (3:21–5:11). Jesus Christ, as the letter to the Ephesians says, "has destroyed the barrier, the dividing wall of hostility" that existed between Jews and Gentiles, and he now presents both Jews and Gentiles "to the Father by one Spirit" (2:11–22).

This being so, by only a slight extension of the principle we may also say that the gospel lays on Christians the necessity of treating all people impartially, regardless of race or culture, with a view to their present good and their eventual redemption. The cultural mandate of the gospel expressly excludes all human notions about respecting people because of race, culture, or merits, whether earned or assumed. Nor does it ask that people be treated as their common humanity deserves. Rather, the cultural mandate of the gospel lays on Christians the obligation to measure every attitude and action toward others in terms of the impartiality and love which God expressed in Jesus Christ, and to express in life such attitudes and actions as would break down barriers of prejudice and walls of inequality, without setting aside the distinctive characteristics of people.

C. THE CHURCH'S PRACTICE IN
THE NEW TESTAMENT

The New Testament accounts of how the early Church implemented the principle "neither Jew nor Greek" are quite mixed, with many uncertainties and some halting starts recorded. It took rather heroic action by Paul to lead the way in this area, and it required quite a bit of heroism on the part of the Jerusalem apostles as well to lend him a measure of support. Yet many in Jerusalem who believed in Jesus seem to have remained either unconvinced as to the legitimacy of the principle itself or uncertain as to how to work it out in practice.

Christians in Jerusalem evidently had no difficulty in accepting that Gentiles were to be included in the promise of the gospel. After all, the inclusion of Gentiles was a recurring theme in the prophetic portions of their Scriptures (e.g., Gen. 22:18; 26:4; 28:14; Isa. 49:6; 55:5; Zeph. 3:9–10; Zech. 8:22). But they appear to have thought of their relations with Gentiles strictly on the basis of a proselyte model, wherein Gentiles would be accepted as fellow Christians only as they professed faith in Jesus as Israel's Messiah *and* related themselves to the institutions of Judaism. In the Old Testament, Israel was the appointed agent for the administration of God's blessings, and only through the nation and its institutions could Gentiles have a part in God's redemption and share in his favor. And there seems to have been no expectation on the part of the earliest Jewish believers in Jesus that this relationship would be materially altered—except, of course, that in "these last days" God was at work in and through Jewish Christians as the faithful remnant within the nation.

Stephen is portrayed in Acts as pleading for a radical recasting of Jewish life so as to make Jesus the Messiah—rather than the Jewish homeland or the Mosaic law or the Jerusalem temple—the center of Israel's thought and worship (Acts 7:2–53). In many ways he was more daring than other Jerusalem Christians, more ready to explore the logical implications of commitment to Jesus, and more prepared to advocate positions which would ultimately minimize the distinctions between Jews and Gentiles in the one Body of Christ. Yet Stephen's purpose, it seems, was to raise a prophetic voice *within* Israel, and Adolf Harnack was probably right to insist that "when Stephen was stoned, he died, like Huss, for a cause whose issues he probably did not foresee."[6] Certainly Stephen's message had far-reaching implications for relations between Jews and Gentiles in the Church. But his martyrdom cut short the development of those implications for the moment, and it is difficult to argue that he himself had in mind any clear conception of a law-free gospel or the direct acceptance of Gentile Christians by Jewish Christians.

Likewise, Peter is presented in Acts as making a distinctive advance in Jewish-Gentile relations through a direct ministry to Cornelius, a Roman centurion stationed at Caesarea (Acts 10:1–11:18). In a vision Peter was instructed to "call nothing unclean that God has made clean" (10:15) and to "make no distinction" between Jews and Gentiles (11:12), and as a result of the Spirit's working he was forced to confess that "God does not show favoritism but accepts men from every nation who fear him and do what is right" (10:34–35). Therefore in his preaching at the home of Cornelius, Peter proclaimed "the good news of peace through Jesus Christ" and spoke of Jesus in universalistic fashion as being "Lord of all" (*pantōn kurios;* 10:36). Yet though the conversion of Cornelius was a landmark in the history of the gospel's advance from its strictly Jewish beginnings to its penetration of the Roman Empire, at the time it was not considered to settle any of the issues facing the Church with regard to Jewish-Gentile relations. Rather, it seems to have been viewed as an isolated and exceptional incident, not as a precedent for a direct outreach to Gentiles or a paradigm for Jewish-Gentile relations within the Church.

It was Paul who first saw clearly the legitimacy of the cultural mandate of the gospel and who first sought to work it out in practice. The realization of the equality of Jews and Gentiles before God came to him, he insisted, "by revelation" (cf. Gal. 1:11–12; Eph. 3:2–6), and was so uniquely his that he spoke of it as "my gospel" (Rom. 16:25–26). While respecting certain historical advantages of one people over another (cf. Rom. 3:1–2; 9:4–5), Paul proclaimed a gospel of "no dif-

---

[6]Harnack, *The Mission and Expansion of Christianity,* I, trans. J. Moffatt (London: Williams & Norgate, 1908), 50.

ference" between Jews and Gentiles in condemnation before God (Rom. 1:18–3:20), "no difference" between Jews and Gentiles in access to God (Rom. 3:21–5:11), and "no difference" between Jews and Gentiles in the one Body of Christ (Rom. 9:1–11:36; Eph. 2:11–22). And it was this gospel that Paul endeavored to express in all his missionary activities and all his pastoral responsibilities. Had he contented himself with a missionary outreach to Gentiles through the old procedures and within the confines of local synagogues, and had he been willing to accept Gentiles strictly on a proselyte basis, early Christianity would have been spared much of the trauma it experienced in its head-on collision with both Judaism and Rome. But Paul's vision was clear as to the equality of Jews and Gentiles, and it was only because of the clarity of his vision and the heroism of his actions that the Christian gospel was seen to be Good News in the Greco-Roman world of that day—and continues to be Good News today.

In the apostolic period it was Paul who led the way in working out this principle of the gospel in the everyday life of the early Church. Peter at Antioch of Syria retreated from such a mandate in his practice, and Paul "opposed him to his face, because he was in the wrong" (Gal. 2:11). "Even Barnabas," Paul says in recounting that same Antioch episode, was unable to see with clarity the implications of the gospel proclamation, and he too proved false to his own principles in what he did (Gal. 2:13). We must not, however, assume that Paul was entirely without support among first-century Jewish Christians, Peter and Barnabas included. It was at the first ecumenical council of the Church, the Jerusalem Council of A.D. 49, that this matter was taken up as the major item on the council's agenda (cf. Acts 15:1–29). And the effect of that meeting of nascent Christendom's leaders was to shift the consideration of "the Gentile question" from that of a proselyte model, wherein converts had also to become Jews, to an eschatological model, wherein converts could be accepted on an equal basis with Jews without becoming Jews or assuming a Jewish lifestyle.[7]

The prophets, of course, spoke of Gentiles coming to Je-

---

[7]On the Jerusalem council, see my "The Acts of the Apostles," in *The Expositor's Bible Commentary*, vol. 9, ed. F. E. Gaebelein (Grand Rapids, Mich.: Zondervan, 1981), 439–51.

rusalem to learn the ways of God so that they might walk in his paths. But Isaiah also alluded to Gentiles accepted by God as continuing to exist as Gentiles in the coming eschatological days, with their salvation not setting aside their national identities (cf. Isa. 2:4; 25:6–7). Therefore James, citing Amos 9:11–12, equates "the remnant of men" in the eschatological days with "all the Gentiles who bear my name" (understanding the conjunction *kai* of verse 17 to be explicative, "even"), with their continued existence as Gentiles presupposed. In the end times, James seems to be saying, God's one people will be composed of two entities: at the core will be a restored Israel, "David's fallen tent" rebuilt; and gathered around restored Israel will be a company of Gentiles, "the remnant of men," who will share in the messianic blessings but continue to exist as Gentiles without necessarily becoming Jewish proselytes. It is this understanding of the prophets' message, James is presented as insisting, that Peter's testimony and Paul's missionary practice affirm (cf. Acts 15:7–12), and therefore the conversion of Gentiles in these last days must be seen not on a proselyte basis but in terms of an eschatological model.

Martin Luther noted that at the Jerusalem council two matters pertaining to the Gentile question were considered.[8] The second matter was practical and had to do with the advisability of Gentile Christians abstaining from certain practices for the sake of the Jewish-Christian mission and Jewish-Gentile fellowship within the Church, and that was approved (cf. the fourfold decree of Acts 15:20, 29). The first matter—and the major issue facing the council—was theological and had to do with the Judaizers' insistence that Gentiles must be circumcised and adopt a Jewish lifestyle in order to be Christians. And on this matter the council refused to side with the Judaizers, but supported Paul. James, speaking on behalf of the council, may not have been prepared to endorse all the details of Paul's missionary policy—and there is no evidence that he expected the Jerusalem Church to follow suit. But he could not oppose the will of God as expressed in both the Church's experience and the Scriptures. Therefore his counsel

[8]"On the Councils and the Church," in *Luther's Works*, vol. 41, ed. H. T. Lehmann (Philadelphia: Fortress Press, 1966), 68–79.

was that Jewish Christians should take no stance against either the equality of Jews and Gentiles in the Church or the furtherance of Paul's missionary endeavors among Gentiles.

When one considers the situation of the Jerusalem Church in A.D. 49, the decision reached by the council must be considered one of the boldest and most magnanimous in the annals of church history. While still attempting to minister exclusively to Jews themselves, Jewish Christians in Jerusalem refused to impede the progress of that other branch of the Christian mission whose every success inevitably meant only further difficulty and oppression for them. Undoubtedly there was some uncertainty within the council regarding various features of the decision, and probably the decision was arrived at only after a great deal of heart-searching and mental anguish. Likewise, there seems to have continued to exist in Jerusalem a group that remained unconvinced and that continued to speak of the ominous consequences of such a stance. But the decision was made, and the malcontents were silenced—at least for a time.

Just how firmly this principle of equality was fixed in the consciousness of early Christians can be seen, to some extent, by the way the canonical evangelists edited their materials to reflect a growing concern for non-Jews, and the way Luke in the book of Acts balances his portrayals of, first, the Christian mission to Jews and, then, the Christian mission to Gentiles. There were, of course, those who attempted to set aside this feature of the gospel's message, either in theory or in practice. Paul was aware of such efforts (cf. Phil. 3:2ff.) and sought to minimize their effects by presenting a gift from his Gentile congregations to Jewish Christians in Jerusalem as an expression of unity (cf. Rom. 15:25ff.; 1 Cor. 16:1–4). But despite reactionary factions within the early Church and occasional setbacks, there was at the heart of the Christian movement during the last half of the first century a consciousness of the equality of Jews and Gentiles before God and a willingness to try to work out such a principle in practice.

D. CHRISTIANS AND JEWS IN SUCCEEDING CENTURIES

Relations between Jews and Christians generally and between Gentiles and Jews within the Church in particular entered a new phase at the beginning of the second century. Christianity's openness to Gentiles and the success of Paul's missionary endeavors had aroused hostility among the Jews. The success of the Church's Gentile mission, coupled with the relative failure of its Jewish mission, meant that Jewish Christians were becoming outnumbered by their Gentile counterparts. The martyrdom of James and the flight of Jerusalem Christians to Pella, together with the disastrous Jewish war against Rome during A.D. 66–70, effectively brought an end to the special status of the Church with the nation Israel, with the result that leadership in the Church passed into the hands of Gentiles. The consolidation of Judaism after A.D. 70 on Pharisaic principles resulted in Jewish Christians being gradually squeezed out of the synagogues—a process formalized by the *Birkath ha-Minim* ("Exclusion of the Heretics") legislation which was brought into effect sometime during A.D. 80–90 and was directed principally against Jewish Christians (cf. Bab Berakoth 28b; Bab Megillah 17b). Finally, in the second Jewish war against Rome of A.D. 132–135, every vestige of Christianity's relationship with Judaism was broken. Thereafter, Gentile Christendom and Rabbinic Judaism stood as two separate religions in the eyes of everyone, and the Church turned its full attention to the task of winning a hearing for the gospel in the Gentile world.

Whereas the proclamation of the gospel had been earlier directed to both Jews and Gentiles, in the second century it was addressed only to Gentiles. And whereas the *adversus Judaeos* polemic of the New Testament was an intra-family device used to win Jews to the Christian faith, in the second century it became anti-Semitic and was used to win Gentiles. Politically, Rome no longer accepted the Jewish religion as a legal religion (*religio licita*) after the wars of A.D. 66–70 and 132–135. Religiously, the Church was ridiculed by pagans for its Jewish roots. Celsus, for example, derisively asked, "Do you not think that you have made the Son of God more ridiculous by sending him to the Jews?" (cf. Origen, *Contra Celsum* 6.78). And many Gentiles evidently agreed. Therefore, in order to bolster its preaching among the Gentiles, the Church in the second century considered it necessary to dissociate itself from Judaism and from Jews. In so doing, however, it renounced that very tenet of the gospel which came to be part of the early Church's consciousness only through much soul-searching and heroic action: that "there is neither Jew nor Greek" in the new reality established by God in Christ Jesus.

With the dimensions of the Jew-Gentile problem radically altered and with the Church's leadership entirely in Gentile hands, two subtle, but theologically significant, changes occurred in the thinking of second-century Christians. In the first place, the remnant attitude which lay behind first-century Christian polemic was exchanged for one of racial antagonism. The distinction between national Israel and spiritual Israel that is made in the New Testament became in the second century a schism between Jews and Gentiles. The Epistle of Barnabas, for example, asserted that it was the uncircumcised Gentiles and not the Jews whom God meant to be the heirs of the covenant (cf. esp. ch. 13). Justin Martyr even denied the Jews the name Israel, declaring that the Gentile Church is really Israel (cf. *Dialogue* 123). And Tertullian found the following justification in the Old Testament for the supremacy of Christians over Jews:

> God promised that out of the womb of Rebecca "two peoples and two nations were about to proceed" [Gen. 25:23]—of course, those of the Jews, that is, of Israel, and of the Gentiles, that is ours. . . . Beyond doubt, through the edict of the divine utterance, the prior and "greater" people—that is, the Jewish—must necessarily serve the "less"; and the "less" people—that is, the Christians—overcome the greater. (*Answer to the Jews* 1)

In the change from a remnant mentality to one of racial antagonism, the Church pressed the Old Testament into a defense of its exclusivism, with the result that Christians began claiming for themselves all the heroes, all the promises, and all the blessings of the Old Testament—leaving for the Jews all the sinners, all the curses, and all the judgments. In so doing, the complementary poles of promise and judgment in the prophets' preaching were split apart: every promise was seen as applicable to the Church, and every judgment read as descriptive of the Jews. Such an interpretive procedure, of course, as Rosemary Ruether observes, "turns the Jewish Scriptures, which actually contain the record of Jewish self-criticism, into a remorseless denunciation of the Jews, while the Church, in turn, is presented as totally perfect and loses the prophetic tradition of self-criticism!"[9]

A second change that occurred in second-century Christian thought was the loss of the concept of Christ as the fulfillment of salvation history. Unable to conceive of revelation as progressive and redemption as dynamic, Christians tended to turn the Old Testament into a static record of Christian doctrine and to deny any real place to the religion of Israel in the development of redemption. To admit that the Old Testament was a preparation for the gospel was to concede antiquity and a measure of legitimacy to the Jews. Thus, because of its desire to press the claims of antiquity and legitimacy for itself, the Church was forced to interpret the Old Testament as the history of Christianity (cf. Tatian, *To the Greeks* 30–36; Eusebius, *Ecclesiastical History* 1.2.1). And to do this, Christians resorted to allegorical exegesis, with the result that the Old Testament was interpreted "spiritually" rather than "carnally" or "corporally," and the loftiest truths of Christianity were discovered in the most banal of historical statements.

At the same time, however, when it was taking its stand in the Greco-Roman world as a religion distinct from Judaism, Christianity also had to deal with a group from within its own ranks led by Marcion of Pontus, who rejected everything having a Jewish flavor—including the entire Old Testament, the God of the Old Testament, and major portions of the New Testament. It was not possible for the Church to accept Marcion's position and remain true to itself. Nor did it want to, for by jettisoning the Old Testament it would also have had to jettison its apologetic arguments from fulfilled prophecy (understood only in a literal sense) and antiquity. It was, therefore, forced by the nature of the circumstances it faced to denounce Judaism's claim on the Old Testament and assert its own claims on these Scriptures. Both Justin Martyr and Tertullian wrote treatises against the Jews on the one hand, and Marcion on the other. For the only way the Church could both discredit the claims of Judaism and assert its own right

[9]Ruether, *Faith and Fratricide: The Theological Roots of Anti-Semitism* (New York: Seabury Press, 1974), p. 131.

to the Old Testament as a Christian book was to dissociate the Jews from their biblical traditions and to insist that it alone was the True Israel.

The argument used by Christians of the second, third, and fourth centuries to drive a wedge between the Jews and their past was that the Jews had forfeited their election as God's people, with the implication being that Gentile Christians had been assigned their place. It is not possible to give the details of that anti-Jewish argument here, nor is it necessary, for it has been done by others.[10] Here it is sufficient to point out that, in effect, the Church answered Jewish exclusivism with "Christian" anti-Semitism, which was a denial in reverse of Paul's argument in his letter to the Galatians and the hard-won decision of the Jerusalem council reported in Acts. And, sadly, it is this kind of response to Jews and Judaism that has largely characterized Christian theology from the second century to the present. As a result, Christians have treated Jews in one of three ways, depending on the particular situations of the day: they have ignored and ostracized them, forced them to convert to Gentile Christianity and conform to Gentile ways, or persecuted them as apostates and seditionists. The story of the Church's treatment of Jews down through the ages is far from pleasant reading. Christians have usually assumed the role of villain, to their great shame and to the discredit of the gospel.

E. SOME IMPLICATIONS FOR TODAY

The central theme of the New Testament, and that to which the Old Testament points as well, is God's redemption of men and women in Christ. It is a message that stresses reconciliation between man and God spiritually. But it also includes the reconciliation of man with man socially and speaks to the relations of Christians in society. Therefore Galatians 3:27–28 declares in confessional fashion both the vertical and the horizontal dimensions of the gospel: "All of you who were united

[10]Cf. R. Wilde, *The Treatment of the Jews in the Greek Christian Writers of the First Three Centuries* (Washington, D.C.: Catholic University Press, 1949); J. Isaac, *Genese de l'antisémitisme* (Paris: Calmann-Levy, 1956); Ruether, *Faith and Fratricide*.

with Christ in baptism have been clothed with Christ. There is neither Jew nor Greek, slave nor free, male nor female, but you are all one in Christ Jesus." The Church no longer faces questions regarding relations between Jews and Gentiles in the same form that it did in the days of Paul and the Jerusalem council. But we as Christians continue to face issues that are equally as important with regard to our relations with Jews and with people of identifiable ethnic minorities, both in the Church and in society. To take the New Testament seriously means that as Christians we must make the gospel principle of "neither Jew nor Greek" the touchstone for our thought and the apostolic practice the paradigm for our action as we seek to apply the Good News of new life in Christ Jesus to the various cultural issues of life today.

Whereas Paul led the way in the earliest days of Christianity to solve the Jewish-Gentile problem, the dimensions of that problem changed in the second century and new answers were called for. The Church of the second century, however, as we have seen, responded to those changed conditions by developing an anti-Jewish polemic which in its racial and ethnic features fostered anti-Semitism. And the Christian Church in the centuries following built on that heritage, with the result that as an institution the Church cannot be said to have a good track record with respect to its treatment of Jews and its relations with Judaism. The enforced segregation of Jewish villages in Eastern Europe, the Spanish Inquisition, the denial of Jews' entrance into Britain for four centuries, the persecutions of Jews under the Russian czars, the Holocaust perpetrated by Nazi Germany—these are but the most prominent examples of an anti-Semitism which first nourished itself on a misguided Christian theology and then was taken over by other interests to work out its awful fury.

Only today, it seems, has "the Jewish question" become a matter of widespread concern within the Christian Church. And only today have questions that individual Christians were asking earlier begun to penetrate the consciousness of the whole Church—questions like the following: Is the New Testament anti-Semitic? What are the theological roots of anti-Semitism? Can Christians be non-Judaic in religion without also being anti-Semitic? Is there a continuing plan and purpose for the nation Israel in the divine economy? Can the Church be open to Jews and Judaism and still maintain its own uniqueness? What is a proper Christian witness to Jews, and how can it be carried out? Must so-called Messianic Jews conform to practices that have developed within the Christian Church over the centuries, or can faith in Jesus be expressed through the forms of Judaism? If God has ordained religious pluralism, how do we as Christians live in such a situation— particularly with respect to Jews and Judaism?

Likewise, it is only recently that the Church has awakened to the presence and needs of ethnic minorities. Before the great missionary outreaches which began only a century ago, Christians largely existed in rather self-contained national en- claves, having little contact with people of other cultures and being unaware of matters having to do with multiculturalism. Even with the rise of the modern missionary movement, is- sues pertaining to transculturalism and multiculturalism were usually left to the missionaries themselves and to the mis- sionary societies which sent them out. In our day, however, the situation is entirely different. With the ease of travel, the worldwide nature of communications, the liberation of en- slaved peoples, and the migrations of many in search of a better life, Western Christendom has been confronted by mul- ticulturalism as never before. Christian theology today can hardly be written without attention to the plurality of religious concepts which all this has brought about. Christian ministry has been compelled to come to terms with what it means to be Christ's own and to proclaim Christ's gospel in the midst of such diversity. And Christian ethics has been faced with the task of thinking through what it means for men and women of diverse cultures to be made one in Christ and of actualizing a Christian understanding of oneness in both the Church and society.

The early Church's doctrine of oneness in Christ cannot be taken to mean the renunciation of racial characteristics or ethnic distinctions. Paul, for example, always considered him- self a Jew—albeit, of course, a fulfilled Jew since his encounter with the risen Christ. He lived a Jewish lifestyle as a Chris- tian, and he counseled his converts to express their Christian faith in accord with the cultural forms with which they were accustomed (cf. 1 Cor. 7:17–20, 24). Oneness in Christ, there-fore, cannot be construed to require the rejection of one's racial identity or the dissolution of one's culture in favor of some supposed monochromatic or monolithic ideal. Rather, it has to do with the setting aside of pride and exclusivism. It is our acceptance of one another because we have been accepted by God, with such acceptance operative in every area of life. Admittedly, we may fail in our expression of the gos-pel's cultural mandate. We may also be misunderstood for trying. But failure or misunderstanding are never reasons for readjusting the principle or discontinuing attempts to put it into practice.[11] In Christ, God has dealt with us in personal and transcultural ways that require from us a response that is also personal and transcultural, not just legal or conventional.

Each of us, of course, is a member of a particular race and has been raised in some particular culture. And each of us has his or her own preferences with respect to race and cul-ture—in the vast majority of cases, preferring what we are and what we have become accustomed to. All of us, to varying degrees, are prejudiced, for we all have deep-seated prefer-ences and tend to class what does not fall within our prefer-ences as less appealing or less worthy. But the gospel calls on us as Christians to set aside all such dwelling upon our pref-erences as would lead to pride and exclusivism, and to rec-ognize our oneness with all Christians in the new relationship brought about by God through Jesus Christ. The Church of the post-apostolic period turned us in a wrong direction in this matter through its anti-racial and anti-ethnic polemic. Similarly, the humanistic spirit of our day has misled us into thinking that mere tolerance of one another is the same as acceptance.

What we need as Christians individually and as the Church collectively is to hear again that clear cultural mandate which

[11]Here I must voice my unhappiness with the "homogeneous unit" principle that has arisen in some quarters of the church-growth movement (cf. Donald A. McGavran, *Understanding Church Growth* [Grand Rapids, Mich.: Eerdmans, 1970]; C. Peter Wagner, *Our Kind of People: The Ethical Dimensions of Church Growth in America* [Atlanta: John Knox, 1979]). While sociological analyses of church growth are valuable, the theology epitomized in the title *Our Kind of People* turns, I'm sorry to say, cultural snobbery into some kind of Christian virtue and success into the dominant biblical principle.

forms part and parcel of the gospel proclamation and which is embedded in Galatians 3:28—that mandate which indeed is part of the "Magna Carta of the New Humanity": that "there is neither Jew nor Greek" in the new fellowship established by God through Christ, "for you are all one in Christ Jesus." And having heard it again, we need to seek by God's Spirit, grace, and power to put it into practice in our day in accordance with the paradigm set by the first-century Church as depicted in the New Testament. It is a word of the gospel which calls for soul-searching, clear thinking, and heroic action. But so it did in the Church of the first century, and we are called to follow that example.

IV. THE SOCIAL MANDATE:
Neither Slave nor Free

Having considered the hermeneutics of New Testament social ethics in the first two chapters and the cultural mandate of the gospel in the third, we now turn to the question of the relevance of the New Testament's proclamation and practice for what is a pivotal issue in all human relationships: the question of slavery and freedom. I have called the New Testament's treatment of this matter the social mandate of the gospel simply because the issue strikes at the heart of every communal relationship and epitomizes the essence of what it means to live societally as humans. In this chapter we will look first at the nature, extent, and effects of slavery in the ancient world. Then we will consider the social mandate of the gospel itself, dealing with the principle as proclaimed in the New Testament and the practice of Christians as depicted in both the New Testament and the records of church history. Finally, as in the previous chapter, I would like to mention some implications for Christian social ethics today.

A. SLAVERY IN THE ANCIENT WORLD

Slavery in the Greco-Roman world was a judicially protected institution. It has been estimated that slaves comprised roughly one-third of the entire population of the empire, with slaves being anywhere from three to five times more numerous than Roman citizens, and slaves and former slaves ("freedmen") together constituting the majority of the population. Seneca tells us that legislation to compel slaves to wear a particular type of clothing to distinguish them from free men was defeated in the Roman senate because it was feared that slaves would then recognize how large and powerful a group they were, and might revolt (*De Clementia* 1.24.1).

Prior to the first century A.D., the major sources of supply for slaves were war and piracy. Slave traders followed the armies and served as middlemen for returning marauders in disposal of their booty. However, with the cessation of Rome's wars of conquest and the establishment of the empire, these sources of supply were almost eliminated. Thereafter the major source was children who had been either abandoned by their parents or sold into slavery. Slave breeding was also practiced. And though there were laws forbidding slavery because of indebtedness (from as early as 326 B.C.), some were still sentenced to slavery for indebtedness; others were made slaves as punishment for their crimes.

Slavery was a recognized part of the Greco-Roman economy, and was increasing rather than declining during the first century A.D. The lives of the middle and upper classes could hardly have gone on without it, so ingrained was it in the fabric of the society. Slave trading was an accepted profession, and slave revolts were seldom successful in the prevailing climate of opinion. Fear of mortal reprisal kept most slaves subservient.

Slaves were often treated humanely, with many faring better than lower-class free men in matters of food, housing, clothing, education, and spending money. There is considerable evidence that large numbers of slaves received their freedom because of the beneficence of their masters, and that as freedmen many became artisans, people of commerce, and even civic leaders. Yet slavery was an oppressive thing for most, shot through with fear, malice, and resentment. Many slaves were severely ill-treated, particularly those working on the land and in mines. And to judge by the statements regarding slavery and the stress on freedom in the *Dissertations* of the Stoic philosopher Epictetus, who himself had been a slave, many would have preferred suicide—if only they had had the nerve—to continued slavery. The most oppressive thing about slavery, of course, was that a slave was considered merely "a thing" (*res*), "a mortal object" (*res mortale*), simply "chattel" (*mancipium*), not a person, and had no personal or human rights except as permitted him by his master.

Slavery in the Jewish world was also an accepted part of the fabric of society, with roots in the legal provisions of the Pentateuch. It was, however, less extensive and less exploitative among the Jews than in the Roman Empire generally. Because of Israel's memory of the agony of her own slavery in Egypt, slaves were generally treated with a greater degree of kindness by Jewish masters, and some human rights were built into the system.

On the basis of Leviticus 25:39–55, Judaism made a sharp distinction between Jewish slaves and Gentile slaves. A Jew might become a slave in restitution for thievery (Exod. 22:3) or because of insolvency (Lev. 25:39). But a Jewish slave was to be treated by his Jewish master "as a hired worker or a temporary resident" (Lev. 25:40, 53)—not ruthlessly, but in the fear of God, with respect for the fact that he was a fellow Israelite, a fellow servant of God, and was also delivered from Eyptian bondage (Lev. 25:42–43, 55). All Jewish slaves, in fact, whether male or female, were to be released at the beginning of the Year of Jubilee, which occurred every fifty years, with compensation given them for the years of service rendered (Lev. 25:40–41, 54). And Jews who sold themselves into slavery were to be released by their Jewish masters in the Sabbath year, after no more than six years of service (Jer. 34:14). There were other grounds for release as well. A female slave, for example, who had been sold on the understanding that she would be married to the master's son was to be set free if he refused her or if he married another wife in addition without providing her "food, clothing and marital rights" (Exod. 21:7–11). Likewise, a relative could redeem a Jewish slave by paying the price of the service yet outstanding, or the Jewish slave could redeem himself on the same basis if he could acquire enough money (Lev. 25:47–52).

Gentile slaves of Jewish masters, however, entertained no such hopes for release. Their service was perpetual, and their condition was inherited by their children (Lev. 25:44–46). While they could expect to be treated with greater kindness under Jewish masters than under Gentile masters, they were nonetheless still considered to be property and could be used in any way their masters saw fit. Only if they were seriously maimed by their masters were they to be automatically set free. Otherwise, the laws governing slavery in the Roman Empire pertained, and they were treated accordingly.

B. THE MANDATE OF THE GOSPEL

When we consider how ingrained the institution of slavery was in the ancient world and how dominant the personal, charismatic, and eschatological features of the gospel were in the consciousness of the earliest Christians, it may seem surprising that social relations between slaves and free men and the status of slaves would even be matters of concern in the early Church at all. Nevertheless, in the "Magna Carta of the New Humanity" of Galatians 3:28, after the phrase "neither Jew nor Greek" appears the phrase "[neither] slave nor free"— a statement, as we proposed earlier, which may have been part of an early Christian baptismal confession. When first used, perhaps most understood the phrase to mean only that the difference between slaves and free men who are "in Christ" is really of no spiritual significance before God—that is, that in their relations with God, all people, whatever their stations in life, can come to God through Christ and be accepted. But the phrase is also pregnant with societal implications. And undoubtedly some early Christians realized, at least to some extent, the importance for society of what they were confessing. From the way in which Paul treats the issues inherent in the expression, it seems evident that he began to appreciate the scope of what is involved in this early confession.

Israel knew God as the God who sets captives free and who commanded his people not to mistreat aliens, for "you yourselves know how it feels to be aliens, because you were aliens in Egypt" (Exod. 23:9; cf. 22:21). Likewise, the Israelites knew themselves to be the people of God because of God's love and faithfulness in delivering them from slavery in Egypt (cf. Deut. 7:7–8). The standard of conduct for the Jew, therefore, was set by God in delivering his people from bondage. Thereafter when Jews asked such questions as "How should I treat the alien? the helpless? the needy? the enslaved?" they were to answer in terms of God's love and faithfulness as manifested in their own history, not in terms of any human measurement. Such considerations, of course, had an ameliorating effect on the practice of slavery in Jewry, particularly in the treatment of Jewish slaves. But with humankind being more influenced by human standards than responsive to the divine example and with implications all too slowly appreciated because of human sluggishness, they did not have their full effect in the Jewish experience.

In like manner, early Christians knew God as the God of love and faithfulness because of his redemption provided in Christ Jesus (cf. Rom. 5:6–8, 10). Thereafter when they asked such moral questions as "How should I treat those who are powerless? without status? in need?" they were to begin their answer by asking, "How did God treat me when he sent his Son to deliver me?" As they had been loved, so they were to love; as they had been forgiven, so they were to forgive. And as they had been released from the slavery of sin, so they were to be partners with God in setting captives free. Thus, when they proclaimed their faith in Christ, they spoke of there being "neither slave nor free" in the fellowship established by God in Christ. Freedom, as they saw it, was a dominant feature and a necessary implication of the gospel. While Jews thanked God that he had not made them boors or slaves (cf. Tos Berakoth 7:18; Jer Berakoth 13b; Bab Menahoth 43b), early Christians, knowing freedom in Christ, proclaimed that one's status in society made no difference before God spiritually, and that what God did in Christ had important significance for relations between slaves and free men societally. In fact, as new people in Christ the early Christians proclaimed a gospel that upheld freedom in both its spiritual and its societal dimensions.

C. THE CHURCH'S PRACTICE IN THE NEW TESTAMENT

Jesus' ministry was dedicated to proclaiming freedom and releasing the oppressed, as his use of Isaiah 61:1–2a at Nazareth makes plain:

> "The Spirit of the Lord is on me;
>   therefore he has anointed me to preach good news to the poor.
> He has sent me to proclaim freedom for the prisoners
>   and recovery of sight for the blind,

to release the oppressed,
to proclaim the year of the Lord's favor." (Luke 4:18–19)

In fact, so dominant was this theme in Jesus' preaching and activity that Luke has placed the Nazareth pericope with this quotation from Isaiah 61 at the very beginning of his two-volume work (Luke 4:14–30; cf. Mark 6:1–6a; Matt. 13:53–58) as the frontispiece and programmatic prologue to all that follows—both in the ministry of Jesus (the Gospel according to Luke) and in the ministry of the Church (the Acts of the Apostles). And John's Gospel captures the essence of Jesus' proclamation in the words: "If the Son sets you free, you will be free indeed" (John 8:36; cf. 8:32).

Our concern, however, is not so much with Jesus' ministry of freedom—though, of course, that is the basis for the distinctive Christian message—as it is with the early Church's practice in explicating its proclamation of freedom. And for this we are drawn immediately to the letters of Paul and find that our investigation is confined almost entirely to Paul. Though making up only about one-fourth of the material in the New Testament, Paul's letters contain over twice as many instances of the noun "freedom," the adjective "free," and the verb "to free" (used twenty-nine times in all) than all the rest of the New Testament together (in which there are thirteen instances in all). In fact, only Paul among the writers of the New Testament uses the language and concept of freedom with any degree of frequency—and then, interestingly, more so in his four great missionary letters (Galatians, 1 Corinthians, 2 Corinthians, and Romans) than elsewhere.[1] Indeed, Paul is rightly called the "Apostle of Liberty," for it was he who led the way in the early Church in spelling out the work of Christ in terms of freedom.

---

[1] Paul uses the noun "freedom" (*eleutheria*) in Rom. 8:21; 1 Cor. 10:29; 2 Cor. 3:17; Gal. 2:4; 5:1, 13 (twice); the adjective "free" (*eleutheros, apeleutheros*) in Rom. 6:20; 7:3; 1 Cor. 7:21, 22 (twice), 39; 9:1, 19; 12:13; Gal. 3:28; 4:22, 23, 26, 30, 31; Eph. 6:8; Col. 3:11; and the verb "to free" (*eleutheroō*) in Rom. 6:18, 22; 8:2, 21; Gal. 5:1. In certain cases the verb "to redeem" (*exagorazō*; Gal. 3:13; 4:5) and the noun "the right" (*exousia*; Rom. 9:21; 1 Cor. 9:4, 5) carry the idea of freedom as well. Elsewhere in the New Testament the noun "freedom" appears in Jas. 1:25; 2:12; 1 Pet. 2:16, 19; the adjective "free" in Matt. 17:26; John 8:33, 36; 1 Pet. 2:16; Rev. 6:15; 13:16, 19; and the verb "to free" in John 8:32, 36.

Yet what strikes us as somewhat strange when reading Paul is that with such an emphasis on freedom the apostle was so relaxed and noncommittal about the institution of slavery itself. Neither in his pronouncements regarding freedom in his four great missionary letters nor in his references to slavery in the Prison Epistles does he speak directly about slavery as an institution. While concerned to break down barriers between Jews and Gentiles because of the gospel's cultural mandate, he seems indifferent to any direct confrontation with the institution of slavery because of the gospel's social mandate. From our twentieth-century Christian perspective on freedom—which has, in fact, been largely formed on the basis of Paul's teaching—we are forced to ask why Paul himself failed to wield the principle of "neither slave nor free" as a mighty sword in warfare against the institution of slavery in his day, much as he used "neither Jew nor Greek" in his battle for the unity of the Church.

A number of reasons have been given by commentators to explain Paul's failure to speak out against slavery per se. One set of explanations stresses the nature of slavery in Paul's day and the huge gap that exists between attitudes toward slavery then and now. As we have seen, slavery was an accepted institution throughout the Greco-Roman world, and its existence was supported among Jews even by biblical law. To attack it as an institution, therefore, was to attack a major structure of ancient society. In the prevailing climate of opinion, that would probably have been as futile as Don Quixote's tilting at windmills. It may even, as C. H. Dodd supposed, "have had the result of provoking the horrors of another servile war."[2] Furthermore, slavery in Paul's Jewish experience was not the vicious thing it was in many other parts of the empire, and in the cities he visited on his missionary journeys it probably often wore the mask of civility.

Yet certainly there was more to Paul's silence than this. The apostle was not adverse to a head-on confrontation with what he saw to be the evils of ethnic exclusivism in his fight for Gentile freedom, and he does not appear to have been the

[2]Dodd, "The Ethics of the Pauline Epistles," in *The Evolution of Ethics*, ed. E. H. Sneath (New Haven, Conn.: Yale University Press, 1927), p. 324.

kind of person to withdraw from a conflict where he believed an important issue of the gospel to be at stake. The pressures of first-century society may explain to some extent the external circumstances for his silence. But we are still left to wonder why, with his lofty principles and his usually incisive mind, Paul never spoke out clearly against the diabolical nature of slavery in treating persons as non-personal entities.

Another set of reasons given for Paul's failure to speak out against slavery focuses on the apostle's own involvements and his priorities. With his interest being primarily in the spread of the gospel among the Gentiles, he saw clearly the evils of an ethnic exclusivism and considered it imperative for the sake of the gospel and the unity of the Church to demolish the distinction between Jews and Gentiles. But not being personally involved with the slavery question, he perhaps did not feel the same necessity to apply the principles of the gospel in this area as he did in the other. Furthermore, in his early ministry he expected the return of Christ to take place soon (cf. 1 Thess. 4:13–5:11), whereas later he had to guard against a developing radicalism in his churches (cf. the Corinthian correspondence and the Pastoral Epistles)—and both his earlier eschatology and his later need to safeguard the faith would have contributed to his conservatism with regard to slavery.

Yet while a knowledge of first-century society sheds light on the external circumstances associated with his silence and an understanding of his own priorities illumines, to some extent, aspects of his rationale, at the heart of Paul's attitude toward the slavery question was a theological perspective which was of great importance to the apostle: that there must first be a "Christ consciousness" before there can be a "Christian consciousness," and that in working out a Christian consciousness, attention must be given to the quality of personal and corporate relationships before dealing with structures as such. Theo Preiss has aptly characterized Paul's view of the gospel vis-à-vis society: "The Gospel penetrates systems and civilizations but is never identified with them. In particular it is more realistic than all idealisms and all so-called political realisms, for it attacks the heart of problems, the personal centre and personal relations."[3] That does not mean that Paul held only to the status quo with respect to society and its institutions. Admittedly, at times he almost sounds like he does, as when he tells the Corinthians, "Each one should retain the place in life that the Lord assigned to him and to which God has called him. This is the rule I lay down in all the churches" (1 Cor. 7:17; cf. vv. 20–21, 24). Yet rather than defending the status quo, "Paul felt," as Peter Richardson notes, "that social institutions as institutions did not deserve first attention. He was interested in relationships, and [believed that] the effects of the chasm between freeman and slave could be bridged by the quality of personal and corporate relationships when both were 'in Christ'."[4]

The way in which Paul emphasized relationships and began to work out the social implications of the gospel in specific situations can be seen in the "house rules" or "house tables" (*Haustafeln*) of Colossians 3:18–4:1 and Ephesians 5:21–6:9. Paul was not the originator of such ethical compilations. Earlier Greek and Jewish moralists had comparable sets—for example, Attalus of Pergamum (as recorded by Polybius, *Histories* 18.41.8–9) and Philo (*De Decalogo* 165–167). And they continued to appear after Paul's day in the writings of Josephus (*Contra Apion* 2.199–210) and the Stoic philosophers Epictetus, Diogenes Laertius, and Pseudo-Phocylides. Yet while comparable in both form and content to other known sets of house rules, those of Paul in Colossians and Ephesians are distinguishable from their predecessors and immediate successors in two important respects.

In the first place, the motive and the basis for ethical practice are different in Paul's house rules than in other extant sets. The advisability for proper action in the Greek house rules is founded on the premise that it is good for oneself, thereby bringing one into harmony with an all-embracing order of the universe. Jewish house rules, of course, rise above such a rationale and relate ethics to the revealed will of a beneficent God who desires the protection of the weak and

---

[3]Preiss, "Life in Christ and Social Ethics in the Epistle to Philemon," in *Life in Christ* (London: SCM, 1954), p. 33.

[4]Richardson, *Paul's Ethic of Freedom* (Philadelphia: Westminster Press, 1979), p. 41.

the unimportant. With Paul, however, the motive and rationale for ethical living within the family focuses on being "in Christ" and "in the Lord." So wives are exhorted to submit to their husbands "as is fitting in the Lord" (Col. 3:18) and "as in the Lord" (Eph. 5:22), children to obey their parents "in the Lord" (Eph. 6:1; cf. Col. 3:20), slaves to serve as though serving the Lord (Col. 3:22–24; Eph. 6:5–7), and masters to treat their slaves in a manner that reflects their own responsibility to their heavenly Master (Col. 4:1; Eph. 6:9).

A second distinguishable feature of the Pauline house rules, and one particularly significant for our discussion here, is the reciprocal nature of the exhortations. In Greek compilations it is the male, adult, and free individual who is addressed and told how to act with respect to his wife, children, and slaves, with the advice given so that he might be able to free himself as much as possible from all ties in order to live in a state of perfect inner harmony. Or, as Eduard Schweizer expresses it: "The aim of the Greek house-tables is the self-protection of the male, adult and free man, who, in order to reach this stage [of perfect inner harmony], should remember the right attitude towards inferiors and their needs."[5] The Old Testament and the Talmud do not have sets of house rules, for it is assumed that the Torah suffices to rule all of family life. It is only when we come to the Hellenized Jew Philo that we get a comparable Jewish formulation, and there in *De Decalogo* 165–167, both husbands and wives, parents and children, masters and slaves are admonished. Yet in Philo, as in the ancient religions generally, it is assumed that all the rights are on one side and all the duties on the other.

In Paul's house rules, however, there is a reciprocal nature to the exhortations, with not only wives, children, and slaves being addressed equally along with their husbands, fathers, and masters (as in Philo's rules but not in the Greek house rules) but also husbands, fathers, and masters being given duties commensurate with those required of their wives, children, and slaves (absent in both the Jewish and the Greek house rules). In so addressing the members of the ancient

[5]Schweizer, "Traditional Ethical Patterns in the Pauline and Post-Pauline Letters and Their Development," in *Text and Interpretation,* ed. E. Best and R. McL. Wilson (Cambridge: Cambridge University Press, 1979), p. 202.

family equally and reciprocally, Paul was, in effect, indicating that the traditional pairings were to be viewed as ethically responsible partners, with each having personal rights, obligations to the other, and obligations to the Lord. He was not, of course, speaking directly against the institution of slavery. Perhaps he felt no urgency to do so, or perhaps he could not see his way clear to do so effectively. But what he did do was to make a start in that direction and to establish the paradigm for a proper Christian response in such matters.

The most significant application of the principle "neither slave nor free" in all the New Testament is to be found in Paul's letter to Philemon regarding the runaway slave Onesimus and his return. Many details of the case are unclear, for the letter only alludes to the circumstances of the case without spelling them out. We don't know, for example, what Philemon's relation to Paul was. All we know is that Paul thought of him as a partner in the gospel and considered Philemon to be in some spiritual debt to him. Nor do we know what occasioned Onesimus' flight or how he came into contact with Paul, nor what happened when he returned to Colosse. It seems difficult to believe that he had been caught by the Roman police and thrown into some common jail with Paul, for Acts suggests that Paul was given preferential treatment while in prison (cf. Acts 28:16, assuming Roman imprisonment as the background for their meeting), and the letter to Philemon presupposes that Onesimus was in Paul's care rather than a prisoner of the state. Probably Ernst Lohmeyer was right in suggesting that Onesimus, having heard of Paul in his master's house and having despaired of further flight, sought out Paul and came to him for asylum, asking for protection and promising to serve him for a specified time in return. He may have originally thought of Paul as some quasi-divine figure, or he may have considered by claiming Paul's protection that he was coming under the jurisdiction of the God whom his master Philemon would recognize. At any rate, coming into contact with Paul, Onesimus became a Christian, and Paul became legally responsible for his welfare and for his return.

Paul could hardly have kept Onesimus with him for long apart from his master's knowledge and consent. Roman law stipulated that anyone who harbored a runaway slave made himself an accomplice to his crime and owed the slave's master remuneration for each day's labor lost. It would also have been inconceivable under Roman law for Paul to have simply assumed the right of ownership over his charge or to have simply set him free. Thus Paul sent Onesimus back to Philemon with this letter asking that he be received back "both as a man and as a brother in the Lord" (*kai en sarki kai en kuriō;* v. 16).

The Letter to Philemon is like a little cameo mined out of the social life of the early Church. In it Paul pleads humbly, though with authority and firm, commanding accent, for Onesimus' reception both as a person and as a Christian. He assures Philemon that whatever Onesimus owes him, he, Paul, will repay. And he reminds Philemon of the spiritual debt he owes the apostle. But nowhere in the letter does Paul speak out against slavery itself or even argue for the emancipation of Onesimus. Some, of course, have asserted that Paul was covertly requesting Onesimus' freedom (e.g., F. Godet and E. Lohmeyer) or have read Paul as asking that Onesimus be made his slave (e.g., J. Knox, proposing also that the request was of Archippus). But the majority of interpreters think not, and I agree with them. Instead, what Paul was doing was pleading that relations between Philemon and Onesimus be put on a basis of mutual acceptance as fellow human beings (*en sarki*) and as brothers in Christ (*en kuriō*), and not merely on a legal or conventional basis. By the fact that Onesimus seems to have returned to his master voluntarily (whatever the hesitancy and reluctance he might have felt), we may surmise that he was prepared to do so, whatever the cost. And the tone of confidence in the letter gives us every reason to believe that Paul had no doubt that Philemon would do likewise.

Rather than engaging in a head-on confrontation with slavery, Paul sought to elevate the quality of personal relationships within the existing structures of society. His insistence on mutual acceptance among Christians, while disparaged by some, was in reality an explosive concept which ultimately could have its full impact only in the abolition of the institution of slavery, for it calls on believers of whatever social status to relate to one another in a manner that transcends the merely legal and the conventional norms. Just what this meant for Onesimus' own place in society we don't know. Perhaps he continued as Philemon's slave but worshipped with his master on an equal basis. Perhaps he was freed by Philemon. Perhaps, as Edgar J. Goodspeed suggested, he later became the Bishop of Ephesus referred to by Ignatius in his letter to the Ephesians (1:1) and so ruled ecclesiastically over Philemon. But whatever his status, we may be reasonably confident that Onesimus' relations with Philemon and Philemon's with Onesimus were considerably altered, being put on an entirely different basis than before—a basis that would ultimately have far-reaching consequences for the institution of slavery itself. Furthermore, evidently because the Church recognized in Paul's words to Philemon the beginnings of a Christian social consciousness and the paradigm for future Christian social action, the Letter to Philemon was preserved and became part of the New Testament canon.

D. THE CHURCH AND SLAVERY IN SUCCEEDING CENTURIES

Attitudes within the Church toward slavery during the Ante-Nicene period are somewhat difficult to assess, simply because of the paucity of source materials and the fact that much of what was written on the subject appears in other contexts. Generally, however, it can be said that in the second century it was widely held by Christians that slaves should be treated kindly and that slavery as an institution did not matter. Like the Stoics, the early Church Fathers were more concerned with the condition of a person's soul than his or her status in life. Second-century Christian writers, therefore, did not speak out against slavery per se. What they were interested in was that Christian masters treat their slaves kindly, that Christian slaves serve their masters faithfully, and that relief be provided for Christian slaves who found life unbearable under unbelieving and tyrannical masters. The Church of the second century seems to have taken seriously Paul's teaching on mutual acceptance of one another, but it went no further than that in working out the implications of the gospel's social mandate for that day. Its treatment of slaves was an advance in social living over the norms of paganism, and the apologists made much of that difference in their arguments for the superiority of Christianity. But second-century Christianity did not seek to go beyond the explicit practice of the New Testament in applying the social principles of the gospel to its own times, perhaps because it viewed conditions to be much the same as they were earlier.

So Ignatius, Bishop of Antioch,[6] in the first extant set of instructions regarding slaves from the post-apostolic period, wrote sometime during A.D. 110–117: "Despise not slaves, whether men or women. Yet let not these again be puffed up, but let them serve more faithfully to the glory of God, that they may obtain a better freedom from God. Let them not desire to be set free at the expense of the common fund, lest they be found slaves of lust" (*To Polycarp* 4.2–3). Ignatius' reference to slaves being "set free at the expense of the common fund" suggests a practice in the Church of ransoming slaves—probably Christian slaves for whom life was unbearable under brutal masters. Yet Ignatius' remark also warns slaves against taking undue advantage of the Church's benevolence. And elsewhere Ignatius evidences his lack of concern for slaves generally by failing to mention them in his listing of the downtrodden and exploited of the earth (e.g., *To the Smyrneans* 6.2).

Second-century Christian leaders owned slaves, as did many others in the Church. Polycarp, Bishop of Smyrna, for example, was arrested when two of his slaves were forced by the Roman authorities to confess that they were Christians and implicated him (cf. *Martyrdom of Polycarp* 6.1–2). The apologists freely acknowledged the ownership of slaves by Christians (cf. Athenagoras, *Supplication for the Christians* 25.1), but they condemned such pagan practices as using slaves for immoral purposes (cf. Justin, *Apology* 2.2) and exposing unwanted infants, for whom there was no other recourse than to be raised as slaves (cf. Justin, *Apology* 2.2; Lactantius, *Divine Institutes* 6.20). Putting the Christian ownership of slaves

[6]Much of the material for this section is taken from Arthur Rupprecht's "Attitudes on Slavery among the Church Fathers," in *New Dimensions in New Testament Study*, ed. R. N. Longenecker and M. C. Tenney (Grand Rapids, Mich.: Zondervan, 1974), pp. 261–77.

in the best possible light, they spoke of slavery as an opportunity for slaves to become Christians under the influence of Christian masters and to witness to their Christian faith by willing service under non-Christian masters (cf. Aristides, *Apology* 15). And they used Christianity's social ethic of mutual acceptance to laud the superiority of Christianity over all other religions. The later apologist Lactantius makes this point most clearly:

> Some will say, "Are not there among you some poor, and others rich, some slaves and others masters? Is not there some difference between individuals?" There is none, nor is there any other cause why we bestow upon each other the name brothers except that we believe ourselves to be equal. For since we measure all human beings not by the body but by the spirit, although the condition of bodies is different, yet we have no slaves, but we both regard and speak of them as brothers in spirit, in religion as fellow slaves. (*Divine Institutes* 6.20)

With the Alexandrian Fathers at the end of the second century, however, a note of prejudice against slaves began to resound in the Church which was a deviation from the theology of mutual acceptance and gave rise to distrust and abuse of slaves by Christians. Slavery was not anywhere as common in Roman Egypt as it was elsewhere in the empire, for Egypt at the time was a relatively poor country which was trying to solve its economic problems by means of serfdom rather than slavery. Nevertheless, there were slaves in Egypt, and Christians owned them as well. Clement of Alexandria, who was prominent in Egypt during A.D. 190–202, spoke frequently about slaves in Christian households, usually with the purpose of warning believers against the dangers of sexual immorality, which he believed too much familiarity with slaves would bring about (cf. *Paidagogos* 3, 4, 7, 9, 11, 12). There is no suggestion in Clement's discussions that he was the least bit concerned about the moral problem of one person owning another person as property. Instead, he speaks of slaves as being servile by disposition and inferior to free men by birth, and concludes that because of their birth they are fit only for servitude. Such a view was in line with the views of Plato, Aristotle, and the Greek classical tradition generally (except the Stoics), but it was a radical departure from the earlier Christian teaching on mutual acceptance.

Origen, who was prominent in Egypt and Syria during A.D. 202–254, also thought of slaves as inferior by birth. In an attempt to justify God and separate slavery from the divine purposes for man, Origen fabricated that damnable heresy about slavery resulting from God's curse on the descendants of Ham—a heresy that has plagued the Church ever since, especially in application to the slavery of blacks. About the Egyptians he says:

> Look to the origin of this race and you will see that their father, Ham, who mocked his father's nakedness, merited that his son Canaan should be a slave to his brothers; so that the condition of slavery should be proof of the wickedness of his disposition. (*Homily on Genesis* 7)

Though he was one of the most brilliant of the early Church Fathers, Origen's writings at this point present a sub-Christian position in their prejudice against slaves because of their birth and God's curse on Ham and his descendants.

Sometime during the fourth century Christians also began to explain slavery as the result of God's judgment on mankind because of Adam's sin, particularly as expressed in Cain's rebellion and God's punishment of Cain, with the result that slavery became viewed as something ordained by God since the Fall. The Greek classical tradition had assumed the natural inferiority of one person to another, but it did not speculate as to why this was so. Christians, however, began to look on slavery as the punishment of God for sin and to expect that this condition would continue to exist until God made all things new at Christ's return. So the only course in this life, they argued, was for Christians to accept the existing social orders and work for tranquillity within and between the orders.

Augustine (c. A.D. 354–430) brought this view to expression at many places in his writings. His Neo-Platonic philosophy, derived from Plotinus, instilled in him a preference for the incorporeal over the corporeal and an indifference to political and civil structures. His Christian theology produced in him a respect for man as a social being, because God made him a social being—yet also a profound consciousness of man as a fallen being, who bears the punishment of sin until God culminates his redemptive purposes at the end of time.

In Book 19 of his *City of God*, Augustine develops at length the theme of man's chief concern being the attainment of eternal life, which is "the supreme good" of life, and argues for the present subordination of society being as God wills it because of both Creation and the Fall. In this present life, Augustine counsels, men should live rightly by faith in response to God in order to inherit that supreme good, and should seek peace and tranquillity within the present orders of society so that they might live happily. "The peace of all things," he writes, "is the tranquillity of order. Order is the distribution which allots things equal and unequal, each to its own place" (19.13). Specifically with regard to the question of slavery, this means (1) that while there is a natural equality of all men because of creation, the introduction of sin into human experience had a profound effect on the relations of men to one another; (2) that slavery is part of the punishment of God for man's sin; (3) that men have lost their primeval bliss and are bound by a host of subordinating relationships; and (4) that the only hope of happiness here and now is to be found in the tranquillity of the orders (see esp. 19.15–16).

Augustine often urged Christians to treat their slaves kindly. John Burleigh aptly summarizes Augustine's counsel: "Towards his slaves the Christian *pater familias* will be kind, and will seek to ensure that, by worshipping the true God now, they will come to the heavenly home where there will be no more slavery or mastery."[7] Yet while Augustine's instincts were eminently humane and his Neo-Platonism tempered by the Bible, he never went so far as to see the Christian faith as any threat to the institution of slavery in this sin-laden age. The only freedom Augustine saw in the gospel for men and women here and now was freedom from the tyranny of sin and the only equality a spiritual equality before God. Otherwise, Augustine sounds very much like Cicero in his prescribed "harmony of the orders" for the social, economic, and political ills of Rome.

At Constantinople, however, sometime around the beginning of the fifth century, what seems to have been a solitary voice was raised against such a view. John Chrysostom (c.

---

[7]Burleigh, *The City of God: A Study of St. Augustine's Philosophy* (London: Nisbet, 1949), p. 173.

A.D. 345–407)—the great preacher of Antioch in Syria and, during A.D. 398–404, Bishop of Constantinople—broke away from the emerging Christian view of slavery, societal orders, and the effects of Christ's work to insist that Christ frees slaves in this life as well as in the next. In a remarkable sermon delivered near the end of his life, Chrysostom said of slavery:

> It is the penalty of sin and the punishment of disobedience. But when Christ came he annuled even this, for in Christ Jesus there is no slave nor free. Therefore, it is not necessary to have a slave; but if it should be necessary, then only one or at most a second. . . . Buy them and after you have taught them some skill by which they may maintain themselves, set them free. I know I am annoying my hearers, but what can I do? For this purpose I am appointed and I will not cease speaking so. (*Homily 40 on 1 Corinthians 10*)

Chrysostom, like his Christian contemporaries, attributed the fact of slavery to God's punishment of sin. Indeed, he frequently drew the parallels between "sin and salvation" and "slavery and freedom" as though the latter couplet had inherent in it some deep spiritual truth. But Chrysostom also reached back beyond the inherited tradition of his day to recapture the principle "neither slave nor free" of Galatians 3:28, and on that basis (though, admittedly, he failed to see in the other two pairings any challenge to the anti-Semitism and male chauvinism of his day) he proclaimed the emancipation of slaves in this life as well as in the next.

It was Augustine's views on slavery, however, that prevailed among Christians until only about a hundred years ago. His interest in the other world and his theology of subordination for this world established, in large measure, the intellectual climate for the Middle Ages. Tying people to their professions or to the land or even to the person of another, therefore, meant very little ultimately, for this life is only a transition to the life to come. John Calvin (1509–1564) adopted Augustine's theology of subordination. And Calvin's Augustinian views on the legitimate division of orders within society were to fall on fertile ground in the seventeenth, eighteenth, and nineteenth centuries, when social and economic conditions seemed to call for the development of a slave system in the New World. Taking their cue from the Portuguese and the Spanish, who had carried on the institution of slavery from Roman times as a consequence of their struggles with the Moors and who introduced Negro slaves into the West Indies and the semitropical regions of the Americas, Dutch and English settlers developed the vast areas of North America in much the same way. Encouraged by the views of Augustine and Calvin on the human condition and its causes, they imported slaves in large numbers from Africa to the New World.

It was only as economic conditions in the northern and western parts of North America made the keeping of large numbers of slaves untenable, and as the humanitarian instincts of the Enlightenment began to emerge, and as Christians began to re-examine their Scriptures apart from an Augustinian preconditioning that slavery as an institution— particularly the enslavement of blacks—was effectively challenged and finally abolished. Only as the Church was able to reach back beyond its inherited tradition was it able to rediscover the truth that social freedom as well as spiritual freedom lies inherent in the Christian gospel.

E. SOME IMPLICATIONS FOR TODAY

Ours is a day when human freedom and human dignity have arisen on the agenda of the world's thought to a place of top priority. And it is entirely right that they have. In the face of various forms of political, social, and economic enslavement, men and women are striking out in hope and frustration against whatever they perceive to be suppressing their legitimate rights as human beings, and are seeking to correct injustices in order to live in freedom and with dignity. Marxism's materialistic ideology, the industrial West's materialistic pragmatism, and the tyranny of various Third World dictators have all contributed to what may be called "The 'Thing-ification' of Man"—that is, to so robbing men and women of freedom and dignity that they not only accept treatment as mere objects but begin to think of themselves as controlled by external forces and devoid of intrinsic worth. The ideological enslavement perpetrated by Marxism is epitomized by such tragedies as the Berlin Wall, the plight of the Vietnamese boat people, and the suppressions in Poland, while B. F. Skinner's *Walden Two* (1948) and *Beyond Freedom and Dignity* (1971) signal the extent to which the mechanization of people can be taken for pragmatic reasons in the Western world. In the Third World, the tyrannical suppression of human rights is grotesquely highlighted by recent events in Chile, Uganda, Iran, and Latin America. These are but the most prominent of many examples that could be cited. Sadly, rather than retreating from the stage of history, the enslavement of people, whether overt or covert, is on the increase today, with new forms being continually invented.

Atheism, of course, lays the blame on religion and insists that only as people are emancipated from the idea of God can they live freely and with dignity. But atheism only substitutes dependence on man for responsibility before God and secularity for religion. And history amply testifies to the inability of naturalistic humanism to provide in practice a sufficient basis for the freedom and dignity it espouses in theory. Indeed, when combined with behavioral psychology, atheism has shown that it frees men and women not only from ideas about God but also from ideas about freedom, dignity, and worth. Emil Brunner was quite right when he said: "For every civilization, for every period of history, it is true to say: 'Show me what kind of god you have, and I will tell you what kind of humanity you possess.' A purely secular civilization will always lack the deeper kind of humanity."[8]

The early Christians, like the Jews, knew their God to be the God of freedom. In their Old Testament Scriptures they read of how he released his people from bondage in Egypt (cf. Lev. 25:39–46); how he removed foreign subjugations when they turned to him (cf. the Book of Judges); how he delivered from Babylonian captivity (cf. Ezra 9:9; Hag. 2:4–5; Zech. 1:16–17); how he instituted the Year of Jubilee (cf. Lev. 25:10); and how he promised a day when his Servant would "proclaim freedom for the captives and release for the prisoners" (Isa. 61:1). At the heart of their consciousness as Christians was the conviction that in Jesus of Nazareth God's promised

[8]Brunner, *Man in Revolt: A Christian Anthropology*, trans. O. Wyon (London: Lutterworth, 1939), p. 34.

Messiah and Deliverer had come (cf. the use of Isa. 61:1–2a in Luke 4:16–21), proclaiming a message of freedom (cf. John 8:31–32, 36) and acting in such a way as to effect mankind's freedom and forgiveness. So they included in their confession of oneness in Christ—a confession which, as we have seen, Paul used in Galatians to support his argument for the equality of Jews and Gentiles—the phrase "neither slave nor free." And though they may not have been able to predict all that this principle of the gospel would effect when put into practice, they were, in fact, proclaiming a truth pregnant with societal implications.

It was the apostle Paul who seems to have been most aware among the early Christians of the societal implications of "neither slave nor free" in the Church's confession—though, admittedly, his perception was not anywhere as clear or his action anywhere as decisive in this area as it was with respect to the principle "neither Jew nor Greek." But that is not to minimize Paul's importance on the freedom question. What he did was to begin to apply this principle of the gospel in ways that were to revitalize some existing structures of society and ultimately to bring about the demise of others.

The Church of the second century, as we have seen, seems to have taken seriously Paul's teaching on the mutual acceptance of one another in Christ, regardless of social status. But it also appears to have gone no further than that in working out the implications of the gospel's social mandate. With the Alexandrian Fathers and the theology epitomized in Augustine, however, the Church veered off in other directions with respect to slavery. It was only as Christians read their Bible apart from these Alexandrian and Augustinian heritages that the institution of the enslavement of blacks was effectively challenged and finally eliminated.

Yet the question of slavery was not entirely settled and put to rest by William Wilberforce's activities in England and by America's Civil War. Like a well-rooted willow, which when cut down at the trunk generates new growth elsewhere in the area, slavery continues in our day in many forms and under a variety of guises. It is imperative, therefore, that Christians constantly be alert and attempt to reapply the gospel's social mandate of "neither slave nor free" wherever such conditions continue to exist—in continuity with the direction set by Paul as he began to apply that same mandate to the circumstances of his day.

The Christian doctrine of oneness in Christ does not mean the end of all social structures or the dissolution of every functional distinction among people. That would be anarchy, not reform, and the gospel is just as much opposed to anarchy as it is to slavery. What the social mandate of the gospel requires of all Christians—both individually and corporately—is that every person be viewed and treated as an individual, with God-given rights, freedom, dignity, and worth; that all overt acts of slavery be opposed in the name of Christ; and that covert and more subtle forms of slavery be identified for what they really are and likewise opposed in the name of Christ. One major problem, of course, is that these latter types of slavery are not as easily identifiable as the more overt forms, and the line between necessary structures and depersonalizing restrictions varies considerably from situation to situation. Who can deny, for example, the need for proper structures in our homes, in our schools, in our churches, and in society? Yet structures can be manipulated to become demonic, robbing people of a truly human existence.

As Christians, we are called upon to preach and teach so that the personhood of every individual is affirmed, and to act in ways that provide a climate for the growth of each individual as a person. As finite and sin-affected people ourselves—who, in addition, are only slowly coming to appreciate the transforming quality and the social implications of the gospel we proclaim—we as Christians often find ourselves confused and divided as to how we should respond in the face of both overt and covert slavery. Nevertheless, we are called as Christians individually and as the Church corporately to hear again that clear social mandate of the gospel embedded in Galatians 3:28: that there is "neither . . . slave nor free" in the fellowship established by God in Christ Jesus. And having heard that gospel principle anew, to seek by God's Spirit, grace, and strength to put it into practice in our day in accordance with the paradigm set for us in the New Testament.

V. THE SEXUAL MANDATE:
Neither Male nor Female

Previously we have dealt with the hermeneutics of New Testament social ethics and then sought to apply those insights and procedures to the issues inherent in the first two parts of the confession of Galatians 3:28: that in Christ Jesus there is "neither Jew nor Greek, slave nor free." In this chapter we will consider what I have chosen to call the sexual mandate of the gospel—that is, the third couplet of the confession of Galatians 3:28: "neither . . . male nor female." Since our discussion here must necessarily deal largely with the status of women, we will look first at the place of women in the ancient world. Then we will turn to the sexual mandate of the gospel itself, dealing with the principle as proclaimed in the New Testament and the practice of Christians as depicted in both the New Testament and the records of church history. Finally, as before, I would like to highlight certain implications for Christian social ethics today.

A. WOMEN IN THE ANCIENT WORLD

The status of women in the Greco-Roman world can be epitomized, by and large, by the second of the "three reasons for gratitude" attributed either to Thales and Socrates by Diogenes Laertius (*Vitae Philosophorum* 1.33) or to Plato by Plutarch (*Marius* 46.1) and Lactantius (*Divine Institutes* 3.19.17), and repeated by Greek men: "that I was born a human being and not a beast, next, a man and not a woman, thirdly, a Greek and not a barbarian." The first-century A.D. Stoic philosopher Epictetus wrote: "Woman's world is one thing; men's another" (*Dissertations* 3.1.24–25; cf. 1.16.19–24).

While the Greek classical tradition often affirmed in principle the equality of women and men, in practice such a status was hardly ever attained. Plato (c. 427–347 B.C.), for example, advocated in the *Republic* that girls be given an education similar to that of boys, and believed that in the ideal state women would participate equally with men in all occupations, including politics and the military. But Plato, as H. C. Baldry reminds us, "was no 'feminist' in the modern sense"; he "always regarded women in general as by nature inferior to men"—not only physically but also intellectually and morally.[1] And though he advocated equality of instruction, Plato himself had only two female students at most (cf. Diogenes Laertius, *Vitae Philosophorum* 4.2). Diogenes also tells us that his own teacher Antisthenes (c. 444–371 B.C.), the founder of the Cynic school of philosophy, coined the aphorism "Virtue is the same for men and for women" (ibid. 6.12), and that Cleanthes wrote a treatise which argued that the gods, men, and women all possess a common virtue because they all partake of a common *logos* (ibid. 7.175). Yet the Greek philosophical school was traditionally, as Henri Marrou points out, a "closed masculine community from which women were excluded."[2] Zeno (c. 336–264 B.C.), the father of Stoicism, also wrote a *Republic* in which he sketched out a utopia where men and women would be equal, even to the wearing of identical clothing (ibid. 7.33)—probably like Crates and Hipparchia, Zeno's teacher and his teacher's wife, who both wore the Cynic's cloak and lived a common ascetic life (ibid. 6.98). Yet none of Zeno's disciples were women. Likewise, the Roman Stoic Musonius Rufus (c. A.D. 25–100) wrote an essay called "That Women Too Should Study Philosophy," in which he advocated a philosophical vocation for women.[3] Yet Musonius' own pupil, Epictetus (c. A.D. 50–138), often spoke of women with contempt, using such adjectives for them as "worthless," "weeping," and "silly" (*Dissertations* 3.24.5, 53;

[1]Baldry, *The Unity of Mankind in Greek Thought* (Cambridge: Cambridge University Press, 1965), pp. 79–80.

[2]Marrou, *The History of Education in Antiquity* (New York: Sheed & Ward, 1956), p. 30.

[3]Cf. C. E. Lutz, "Musonius Rufus, 'The Roman Socrates,'" *Yale Classical Studies*, 10 (1947), 38–43.

cf. 2.4.8–11). And even the noble Roman Seneca (c. 4 B.C.–A.D. 65) was not above referring to women in this way, classifying them as innately inferior to men.[4] As a matter of fact, as Charles Carlston points out in his summary of what he calls "this farrago of nonsense" on the part of ancient writers, while there are occasional positive sayings about women in the literature of antiquity,

> on balance . . . the picture drawn is a grim one. Women, if we were to trust the ancient wisdom, are basically ineducable and empty-headed; vengeful, dangerous, and responsible for men's sins; mendacious, treacherous, and unreliable; fickle; valuable only through their relationships with men; incapable of moderation or spontaneous goodness; at their best in the dark; interested only in sex—unless they are with their own husbands, in which case (apparently) they would rather talk. In short, women are one and all "a set of vultures," the "most beastly" of all the beasts on land or sea, and marriage is at best a necessary evil.[5]

Of course, some women in the Greco-Roman world, on the basis of their own abilities and the shrewd exercise of those abilities, did rise to prominence and positions of authority. The wives of the Diadochoi often overshadowed their men in their exercise of political power, thereby bringing to life the extraordinary female characters of Euripides' tragedies. Women left with an inheritance were sometimes able to exercise considerable influence through the patron-client system that pervaded Roman society. A few women became prominent in business. And outstanding women athletes were included in the Greek games, as, for example, the three daughters of Hermesianax of Tralles, who won prizes at the Isthmian, Pythian, Nemeian, and Epidaurian games during the years 47–41 B.C.—thereby recreating the legend of Atalanta, who became the prototype of the superior woman athlete. But such feats, whether political, economic, or athletic, did little to dispel the dominant male chauvinism of the times.

Only in the teachings of Epicurus (c. 341–270 B.C.) and in the communes of the Epicureans were women both theo-

---

[4]Cf. J. N. Sevenster, *Paul and Seneca* (Leiden: Brill, 1961), pp. 192–96.

[5]Carlston, "Proverbs, Maxims, and the Historical Jesus," *Journal of Biblical Literature*, 99 (1980), 95–96.

retically and actually accorded equal status with men in the Greco-Roman world. But Epicurus' denials of the afterlife and of the gods' influence on human affairs in this life, together with his pessimism regarding the necessity for either public order or marriage, were viewed by the vast majority of people in that day as being much too radical. And his doctrine of happiness was seen by most as a specious plea for hedonistic pleasure, with the result that his advocacy of the equality of the sexes was considered both philosophically suspect and practically dangerous—though, sadly, an anonymous version of Epicurus' thought seems to dominate contemporary secular society and to be the most often heard rationale for the equality of the sexes today.

In the Jewish world, where the basic unit of society was the family, the status and worth of a woman were directly related to her place in the family. The unmarried girl was under the authority and protection of her father. It was a relationship of kinship and love, not ownership, and so she enjoyed a status higher than that of a slave. Yet her position was lower than that of her brothers, particularly with respect to education, worship, and inheritance. The marriage laws of Israel gave women an honorable and protected place, yet one that was circumscribed and decidedly subordinate to that of their husbands. A married woman's role was essentially that of a homemaker and a mother, with her praise coming through the wisdom, influence, and exploits of her husband and sons. Despite such heroines as Deborah, Esther, and Judith, in all its historical periods Israelite society was dominated by the male.

The praise of national heroes in Sirach 44–50, for example, is devoted entirely to the praise of "famous" or "pious" men (cf. also 1 Macc. 2:51–60; 4 Macc. 16:20–23), without any mention of women. The covenanters of Qumran shunned the company of women, thereby in their celibacy asserting the supremacy of the male before God. And Philo of Alexandria, though Hellenistic in much of his thinking, seems to have been even more chauvinistic in his views on women than Judaism generally. For him, the proper relation of a wife to her husband was epitomized in the verb "to serve as a slave" (*douleuein*), and the only purpose of marriage was procreation.

Likewise, the Talmud has a number of statements—which appear even in its most noble tractates—that depreciate the place and worth of women, as the following examples show: "He that talks much with women brings evil upon himself and neglects the study of the Law and at last will inherit Gehenna" (Mish Aboth 1:5); "Every man who teaches his daughter Torah is as if he taught her promiscuity" (Mish Sotah 3:4); "Let the words of Torah be burned up, but let them not be delivered to women" (Jer Sotah 19a); and "All we can expect of them [women] is that they bring up our children and keep us from sin" (Bab Yebamoth 63a).

Admittedly, women in ancient Jewry were often treated better than such statements would suggest. And some rose to positions of great prominence within the nation. At one time the Jews even had a woman ruling over them, the shrewd and ruthless Hasmonean queen Salome Alexandra, who reigned during 76–67 B.C. after the death of her husband Alexander Jannaeus. And the New Testament speaks of the Jewish proselyte Lydia (Acts 16:14ff.) and the Jewess Priscilla (Acts 18:2ff.) as being active in commerce. Yet despite such exceptions—and Jews have never been so rigid in their thinking as to prohibit "exceptions"—nowhere in ancient Judaism was there any real endeavor to propose or practice the social equality of the sexes. While the family may have often been matriarchal in flavor because of the strong personality of the wife and mother, Jewish society was always avowedly patriarchal. In the synagogues, for example, women were separated from the men by a screen and allowed to take no part in the service, except, at most, on one occasion yearly, to read one of the lessons (cf. Tos Megilla 4:11; Bab Megilla 23a). And in the Jewish home it was the father who instructed in the Torah and led his family in worship.

B. THE MANDATE OF THE GOSPEL

The boldest statement in all the New Testament on the equality of women with men before God is part three of the confession found in Galatians 3:28: that "in Christ Jesus" there is "neither . . . male nor female."[6] It appears in what has been called "The Magna Carta of the New Humanity," which proclaims that in the new fellowship established by God through Christ, Jews and Gentiles, slaves and free persons, men and women have been brought into a relationship of oneness such as they had not experienced before. Perhaps, as we proposed earlier, this tripartite confession originated in a baptismal liturgy of the early Church. From the way Paul brings in these three pairings—that is, almost unconsciously, as though there was some inseparable relation between them, when only the first is directly relevant for his argument in the Galatian letter—we can affirm that for Paul, at least, these three couplets spoke with meaning to three areas of life where the gospel had a particular social impact for first-century Christians.

It may be that at times after writing Galatians (here assuming a "South Galatian" provenance), Paul felt some hesitancy or uncertainty about the application of the principle "neither male nor female" with respect to certain situations in his churches, as his omission of the phrase in 1 Corinthians 12:13 and Colossians 3:11 seems to suggest and his counsel in 1 Corinthians 14:34–36 and 1 Timothy 2:11–15 may indicate. I will explore these matters more fully when I discuss the Church's practice in the New Testament. But the extremely important point to note here is that when addressing his Galatian converts and when spelling out those new relationships which are meant by God to exist in the fellowship established by God in Christ Jesus, Paul explicitly says that in the same way that Jews are to have no exclusive privilege over Gentiles and free men to have no exclusive advantage over slaves, so men are to have no exclusive prerogatives over women. Many Christians of the first century, of course, may have thought of this new reality and these new relations only in spiritual terms. But Paul speaks in Galatians without any qualification or reservations. His proclamation is a message of freedom and equality that has both spiritual and social dimensions, both vertical and horizontal implications.

[6]The change of *oude* ("nor") to *kai* ("and") in this third couplet is a result of the influence of Gen. 1:27—"he made them male *and* female"—but has no effect on the meaning.

C. THE CHURCH'S PRACTICE IN THE NEW TESTAMENT

The practice of the early Church as to the relation of the sexes appears from the portrayals in the New Testament to be somewhat diverse—even, in fact, contradictory. All of the explicit statements about women are to be found in Paul's letters, though the Gospels and Acts also reflect attitudes of first-century Christians as well. Many interpreters, of course, have been convinced that Paul's view of women was basically a chauvinistic one. Others, however, like Robin Scroggs, insist that "it is time, indeed past time, to say loudly and clearly that Paul is, so far from being a chauvinist, the only certain and consistent spokesman for the liberation and equality of women in the New Testament," and that "he probably inherited this affirmation of equality from the earliest church"[7]— though, interestingly, such a laudatory statement is usually able to be made only after having discarded Ephesians, Colossians, and the Pastoral Epistles from consideration and after declaring 1 Corinthians 14:33b–36 a post-Pauline gloss as well, as does Scroggs.[8] But both the disparaging and the laudatory evaluations of the early Church's practice with respect to women err in their treatments of the New Testament in that they both are selective in their use of the data, and fail to apply a developmental hermeneutic in understanding the data. In what follows, I would like to sketch out an understanding of the New Testament evidence that incorporates such a developmental approach. In so doing, we will be giving attention as well to the circumstances faced by the early Christians in their efforts to work out the principles of the gospel and put them into practice.

The attitude of Jesus toward women is portrayed in our four canonical Gospels as being different from that of his contemporaries, whether Greek or Jewish. As Carlston notes, all of the ancients' "so-called wisdom [about women] is totally absent from the traditions about Jesus": "Jesus was perfectly at ease in the company of women" since "for him equality

---

[7]Scroggs, "Paul and the Eschatological Woman," *Journal of the American Academy of Religion,* 40 (1972), 283.

[8]Scroggs, "Paul and the Eschatological Woman," p. 284.

between the sexes was not so much a distant legislative goal as a rather self-evident fact."[9] He had women followers who learned from him, traveled with him at times, and supported him financially (cf. Luke 8:2–3). He frequently ministered to women—for example, he healed Peter's mother-in-law (Mark 1:29–31, par.), he exorcised a demon from the daughter of a Syrophoenician woman (Mark 7:24–30; Matt. 15:21–30), he raised Jairus' daughter from the dead (Mark 9:18–19, 23–26), he healed the woman with a pernicious hemorrhage (Mark 9:20–22), he raised a widow's son at Nain (Luke 7:11–17), he taught Mary and Martha in their home at Bethany (Luke 10:38–42), and he healed a crippled woman in a synagogue (Luke 13:10–17). As we have seen, many rabbis of the day doubted the ability of women to learn Torah and depreciated their worth. But Jesus' attitude was totally different. By the mere fact of granting women the right to learn the Good News of the Kingdom and to participate in his ministry, Jesus imparted to women a new dignity and role. In so doing, he set a pattern for all his followers individually and for the Church corporately.

In what may be the earliest extant ecclesiastical statement of the Christian Church—namely, the confession incorporated by Paul in 1 Corinthians 15:3b–5, with its fourfold declaration concerning our Lord's death, burial, resurrection, and appearances—there is no mention of women as witnesses. And this, despite the fact that Mark's Gospel would later highlight their presence at the crucifixion and entombment (15:40–41, 47) and their witness to the resurrection (16:1–8). The testimony of women carried little weight in Judaism, and it was evidently for that reason that they are not included in this earliest extant confession of the Church. But such an attitude did not become entrenched among the early Christians, and soon we find them attempting to express a new attitude toward women—one that sprang, we believe, from Jesus and the principles of the gospel.

The letters of Paul are particularly instructive in this regard, for Paul speaks directly to situations having to do with the relation of the sexes in the family and the status of women

---

[9]Carlston, "Proverbs, Maxims, and the Historical Jesus," pp. 96–97.

in the Church. In 1 Corinthians 7 he answers questions put to him about marriage by some members of his Corinthian congregation, and his replies focus on issues having to do with sexuality. Yet in treating these matters he also broadens the discussion to deal with almost the total spectrum of male-female relationships within the family. And, significantly, in dealing with these issues he emphasizes the equality that exists between the sexes and the mutual obligations they have to one another.

Thus with regard to marriage Paul says in 1 Corinthians 7 that "each man should have his own wife, and each woman her own husband" (7:2); and with regard to sexual intercourse within marriage that "the husband should fulfill his marital duty to his wife, and likewise the wife to her husband" (7:3). Again, in speaking of the mutuality of conjugal rights, he says, "The wife's body does not belong to her alone but also to her husband. In the same way, the husband's body does not belong to him alone but also to his wife" (7:4). And he advises them to abstain from sexual intimacy only "by mutual consent" and that only for a limited time (7:5). With regard to divorce, he cites Jesus to the effect that "a wife must not separate from her husband" and "a husband must not divorce his wife" (7:10–11). On mixed marriages, he counsels believers to remain with their unbelieving spouses if at all possible, stating, in carefully balanced fashion, "If any brother has a wife who is not a believer and she is willing to live with him, he must not divorce her. And if a woman has a husband who is not a believer and he is willing to live with her, she must not divorce him. For the unbelieving husband has been sanctified through his wife, and the unbelieving wife has been sanctified through her believing husband" (7:12–14). Likewise, in discussing questions about finalizing engagements, Paul's words concern equally the unmarried man and the unmarried woman (cf. 7:28, 32–34). It would have been easy for Paul, in keeping with the times, to have reserved all of the rights for men and to have laid all of the responsibilities on women. In 1 Corinthians 7, however, Paul speaks of men and women in the family as being accountable to one another in commensurate ways, with both possessing rights and obligations.

We have observed this emphasis on mutuality within the family in Chapter Four when dealing with slave and master relations in the "house rules" of Colossians 3:18–4:1 and Ephesians 5:21–6:9. It is the reciprocal nature of the exhortations and the commensurate duties enjoined upon the various members that set apart Paul's statements there from the vast majority of the "house rules" of antiquity. Now, with regard to relations between wives and husbands, wives are exhorted in these Pauline "house rules" to "submit to your husbands" and husbands to "love your wives." To some, of course, any idea of wives' submission smacks of male chauvinism. Yet Paul evidently thought of submission more broadly and as in some sense a mutual responsibility of all members in the Christian family, for all the exhortations of Ephesians 5:21–6:9 are subsumed under the caption "Submitting to One Another Out of Reverence for Christ" of 5:21—with the verb "to submit" that appears in our English versions at 5:22 in connection with wives actually only picked up from the adverbial participle "submitting" (*hupotassomenoi*) of 5:21.

In his exhortations to spouses in the letters we know as Colossians and Ephesians, Paul seems to be working from two important categories of thought: the category of creation, which often included that of curse as well; and the category of eschatological redemption. It was generally held by Jews that women have been assigned a secondary role in the family because of their derivative creation (cf. Gen. 2:18–25) and because they are more easily tempted to sin than men (cf. Gen. 3:1–7). And Paul seems to take such views for granted. Yet Paul also brings into the consideration of relations between spouses the category of redemption, urging that wives act "as is fitting in the Lord" (Col. 3:18) or "as to the Lord" (Eph. 5:22), and that husbands love their wives "just as Christ loved the church and gave himself up for her" (Eph. 5:25–29). And it is on this latter basis that he speaks of mutuality between husbands and wives, with reciprocal exhortations and commensurate duties given.

In 1 Corinthians 11:2–16 Paul is faced with a practical problem regarding the decorum of women in worship. Apparently some women in the Corinthian congregation, as an expression of what they considered to be their rightful Christian freedom, were flouting certain cultural conventions and in the process causing the Christian gospel to be confused with paganism. Perhaps their enthusiastic praying and prophesying with hair hanging loose was all too reminiscent of the behavior of pagan prophetesses giving voice to their oracles in disheveled frenzy. Or perhaps their appearance in the congregation with hair cut short and heads uncovered was all too suggestive of the styles of the city's prostitutes, who advertised their profession in such a manner. Commentators vary widely in their understanding of the background of the problem. What is obvious, of course, is that the problem of the decorum of women in worship was a real problem among Christians at Corinth, for they sought Paul's advice about it. But what is not always sufficiently recognized is that it was a problem precisely because women were taking a responsible part in the public worship of Christians at Corinth—and, evidently, with Paul's blessing. It was not the fact of a woman praying or prophesying in the congregation that was in question, but the manner in which such activities were to be carried out in light of the circumstances of the day.

Paul's answer to the question put to him is expressed in a series of four arguments. He begins by appealing to the order within the Godhead and within creation: "The head of every man is Christ, and the head of the woman is man, and the head of Christ is God" (v. 3, with evident reference to Gen. 2:21–25). On the basis of this order found within the Godhead and in creation—and moving back and forth in his exposition between a metaphorical and a literal meaning for the word "head" (*kephalē*)—he argues that a woman's decorum in worship should be honoring both to God and her husband (vv. 4–9), and that "the woman ought to have a sign of authority on her head" (v. 10b). Yet it is important to note that while he argues for order and decorum in the congregation on the basis of the order within the Godhead and in creation, he also insists on the basis of eschatological redemption that "in the Lord, however, woman is not independent of man, nor is man independent of woman," and that both together find their source in God (vv. 11–12). What Paul appears to be saying, in effect, is that though he has argued on the basis of creation for the subordination of women in worship, on the basis of redemption he must also assert their equality. Created distinctions did not mean, for Paul, differing value judgments of an ontic (i.e., "as to being") nature regarding men and women. Nor, it may be added, were even functional distinctions always rigidly held to by Paul. Witness, for example, the doxology of 2 Corinthians 13:14, where "the grace of the Lord Jesus Christ" appears before "the love of God"—thereby tempering the seemingly rigid order of the Godhead set out in 1 Corinthians 11:3 ("the head of Christ is God") with the redemptive order of 2 Corinthians 13:14 ("the grace of the Lord Jesus Christ, and the love of God, and the fellowship of the Holy Spirit").[10]

In the midst of this first argument from order, Paul inserts another: "because of the angels" (v. 10a). Just what he meant by this has been hotly debated. Presumably he was asking that things be done decently and in order because of the presence of angels in the meetings of the Corinthian Christians, much as at Qumran everything was to be done properly in preparation for the eschatological battle and no defiled person was to be allowed to join their ranks "because holy angels march with their hosts" (1QM 7.6). Then, in the third place, Paul argues, much like the Stoics, from "the very nature of things" (*hē phusis autē*) in support of his thesis regarding propriety (vv. 13–15). Finally, he argues from the custom of the churches in general (v. 16)—probably having in mind not only the churches of the Gentile mission but also the church at Jerusalem.

Now, all of these arguments are very interesting, and commentators have spent a great deal of time explicating their nuances. I believe that all of them as used by Paul in 1 Corinthians 11 are basically *ad hominem* arguments—that is, meant to appeal to his converts' interests and emotions in terms they would understand (even though much of their background and imagery may be lost to us). But more im-

---

[10]Some who want to hold to fixed orders in the Godhead and/or construct their theology primarily in terms of orders of creation have difficulty with the redemptive order of this doxology. I've known ministers who constantly rephrase it to make it more "theological." But Paul attempted in his thinking and preaching to bring both orders together—though always, I would insist, with an emphasis on the redemptive. So "The Grace" has become the distinctive doxology of the Christian Church.

portant, it need be noted that these arguments build up to and conclude with statements about a woman's covering for her head (specifically vv. 10b, 13–15), and that Paul regards such a covering as the woman's "authority" (*exousia*) to pray and prophesy in the assembled congregation of Christians. Whatever may be said about the nature of the covering for the woman's head, it is most significant for our purposes to observe that Paul assumes that she has the right to pray and to prophesy in the Corinthian congregation when she has this "sign of authority on her head" (v. 10). Whereas Jewish women were screened off from worship and allowed little or no part in the services, Christian women were accorded the freedom to take a responsible part in the services of the Church—a part that was, as F. F. Bruce rightly says, "a substantial step forward in the practical outworking of the principle that in Christ there is neither male nor female."[11]

Likewise, Paul's greetings to his fellow workers in Romans 16 indicate something of his attitude toward women in the Church. Among the persons greeted by name, six are women, and all six are spoken of as having participated in Christian ministry. Phoebe is mentioned first in the list (vv. 1–2), and is called both a *diakonos* (i.e., a "deacon" or "servant") and a *prostatis* (i.e., a "protector" or "patron"). Whether or not these words were at this time technical designations for formal offices, it is clear that Phoebe was an important person in the church at Cenchrea and that Paul recognized her importance. Prisca, or Priscilla, along with her husband Aquila, is greeted next and identified as one of Paul's "fellow workers in Christ Jesus" (v. 3). From the fact that she is listed here before her husband (cf. also Acts 18:18–19, 26; 2 Tim. 4:19), it may be surmised that either she came from a higher social class than Aquila (perhaps she was a Jewess from a family possessing Roman citizenship) or was for some reason considered more important by Christians in the advance of the gospel, or both. Mary, Tryphena, Tryphosa, and Persis are also greeted, with each being commended for having worked hard in the service of Christ (vv. 6, 12). In addition to this

11"'All Things to All Men': Diversity and Unity and Other Pauline Tensions," in *Unity and Diversity in New Testament Theology*, ed. R. A. Guelich (Grand Rapids, Mich.: Eerdmans, 1978), p. 95.

listing, Paul speaks in Philippians 4:2–3 of Euodia and Syntyche as "women who have contended at my side in the cause of the gospel, along with Clement and the rest of my fellow workers." We will probably never know exactly what any of these women did in the churches to merit Paul's commendation. But it seems incontrovertible from these references that women worked alongside men in the Pauline churches and that they did so with Paul's approval.

So far in our treatment of Paul's attitude toward women we have emphasized features having to do with mutuality and equality in his letters, both as regards women in the family and women in the Church. But we have also alluded to statements having to do with submission and subordination. The house rules of Colossians and Ephesians, for example, exhort wives to submit to their husbands, and the argument from the order of creation in 1 Corinthians 11 speaks of subordination. More explicitly, two passages in the Pauline corpus highlight the feature of a woman's submission—even going so far as to command women to be silent in the assembled congregation of Christians. The first is 1 Corinthians 14:34–35:

> Women should remain silent in the churches. They are not allowed to speak, but must be in submission, as the Law says. If they want to inquire about something, they should ask their own husbands at home; for it is disgraceful for a woman to speak in the church.

The second passage is 1 Timothy 2:11–15:

> I do not permit a woman to teach or to have authority over a man; she must be silent. For Adam was formed first, then Eve. And Adam was not the one deceived; it was the woman who was deceived and became a sinner. But women will be kept safe through childbirth, if they continue in faith, love and holiness with propriety.

It is fairly easy to focus attention on those passages that speak of mutuality and equality to the exclusion of those that speak of submission, subordination, and silence—or, conversely, on those that speak of submission, subordination, and silence to the exclusion of those that speak of mutuality and equality. But both are there, and I believe both must be taken into consideration.

To understand Paul on these passages which speak of the submission, subordination, and silence of women, we must keep four matters constantly in mind. We have spoken of each of these at various places earlier, but now must bring them to bear on the discussion at hand in a collective fashion. The first has to do with the question of where one should begin and from what vantage point view the data. And on this we have argued throughout this book that one must begin with the gospel as proclaimed by the apostles and the principles derived therefrom—particularly, with regard to the relations of Jews and Gentiles, slaves and free persons, men and women, one must begin with the confession of Galatians 3:28. As F. F. Bruce says in commenting on this verse: "Paul states the basic principle here; if restrictions on it are found elsewhere in the Pauline corpus, . . . they are to be understood in relation to Gal. 3:28, and not *vice versa*."[12] A second matter to be kept in mind is the developmental nature of Christian thought and expression as portrayed in the New Testament. This means that while we may not be able to draw lines of continuous increase in the understanding and application of gospel truth— or, conversely, lines of devolution (as some would have it)— we must not suppose that everything in the New Testament is uniform either in perception or practice. Third, we need to be conscious of the fact that in seeking to work out the principles of the gospel for his day, Paul and his colleagues seem to have been working from two important categories of thought: that category of thought which emphasizes what God has done through creation, wherein order, subordination, and submission are generally stressed, and that category which emphasizes what God has done redemptively, wherein freedom, mutuality, and equality take prominence. Finally, we need to keep in mind the effect of circumstances the early Christians faced in their efforts to work out the principles of the gospel and put them into practice in various situations. We may not always be able to spell out the precise nature of the circumstances encountered in each case, simply because the texts themselves do not tell us and our knowledge of the

[12]Bruce, *Commentary on Galatians* (Grand Rapids, Mich.: Eerdmans, 1982), p. 190.

times is incomplete. But we need always to allow for such a circumstantial explanation before concluding that contradictions exist or trying to explain every difference on a theological basis.

So, for example, when we look again at the house rules of Colossians 3:18–4:1 and Ephesians 5:21–6:9 and study once more the argument of 1 Corinthians 11:2–16, we can see how all four of these matters come into play. We must, we have argued, first of all take our stand with the gospel proclamation and its principles (i.e., with the confession of Galatians 3:28) and seek to understand these passages from that perspective, and not vice versa. Then we need to be prepared for variations in perception and practice in the outworking of the gospel, allowing as well for developments in both the understanding and the expression of what that gospel means. Further—and particularly in view of the fact that in these passages Paul affirms the mutuality and equality of the sexes while also speaking of the submission and subordination of women—it is important to recognize that in his treatment of women Paul seems to be attempting to bring together two important theological categories: the redemptive category of new life in Christ wherein freedom, mutuality, and equality are prominent, and the category of what God has done by means of creation wherein order, submission, and subordination are features. Finally, it is necessary to take into consideration the circumstances of the situation, as far as these can be determined, for the apostle was attempting to work out the gospel in the context of particular needs and a particular situation, and not just abstractly. Thus, while vitally conscious of the freedom that is the Christian's because of relationship with Christ and desirous of making that freedom a living reality in the experiences of his churches, Paul was also alert to the dangers of alienating Jews and confusing Gentiles by appearing to be too radical. As Peter Richardson says regarding Paul's argument in 1 Corinthians 11:2–16:

> In order not to sever all relationships with the Jewish community, Paul advises some concessions, mostly at the level of practices inherited from the oral tradition of Judaism. He wishes to keep himself and the Corinthians sufficiently within Jewish norms to maintain a distinction from the prevailing Greco-

Roman behavior. Confusion with Hellenism might occur if women no longer respected the primacy of their husbands. It would not do for a Christian woman to be mistaken for a heathen woman, nor to assert such a degree of freedom that she would be confused with the prostitutes, whether cultic or commercial, who were rather common in Corinth. Too much sexual freedom would create problems for the church's mission to Jews and associate it with the Hellenistic mystery religions.[13]

And what was true with respect to the effect of circumstances on Paul's argument in 1 Corinthians 11 must also be seen to have been true for the way in which Paul formulates his house rules in Colossians and Ephesians, even though we may not be able to spell out the nature of those circumstances with precision.[14]

To appreciate that circumstances played a part in the wording of 1 Corinthians 14:34–35 and 1 Timothy 2:11–15— whether these passages were written by Paul himself, were penned on his behalf by an amanuensis or secretary, or are to be credited to a later Paulinist—is, I would argue, of great importance. Indeed, unless some such circumstantial explanation be appealed to, it is extremely hard to believe that the same man who assumes the right of women to pray and prophesy in the congregation when they do so with decorum considered proper in that day (as argued in 1 Cor. 11:2–16) also wrote that "women should remain silent in the churches" (as argued in 1 Cor. 14:34–35). So we must believe—unless we can espouse some new partition theory for the letter or separate authorship for the passage, which we can't—that Paul's words here pertain to the topic of charismatic excess discussed in chapters 12–14, are meant to restrict certain aberrations which arose within the worship of the Corinthian church, and should not be turned into a general ecclesiological principle that flies in the face of the confession of Galatians 3:28 or the assumption underlying 1 Corinthians 11:5ff. And likewise with respect to 1 Timothy 2:11–15. For though some

[13]Richardson, *Paul's Ethic of Freedom* (Philadelphia: Westminster Press, 1979), p. 68.

[14]One fruitful suggestion takes into account the concentration of gnostic-type terms in Col. 1:15–20 and the argument against sexual abstinence in Col. 2:20–23 to propose that "Wives, submit to your husbands, as is fitting in the Lord" of Col. 3:18 primarily refers to combating certain ascetic and celibate features of the Colossian heresy.

have elevated "I do not permit a woman to teach or to have authority over a man" (v. 12) to the status of a gospel principle, it undoubtedly should be taken more contextually and circumstantially.[15]

That Paul was influenced by circumstances and framed his words to meet specific situations, however, is not to deny that in 1 Corinthians 11:2–16, the house rules of Colossians and Ephesians, and, particularly, 1 Corinthians 14:34–35 and 1 Timothy 2:11–15 there are statements that assert the subordination of women, exhort wives to submission, and command women to be silent in the churches. While recognizing that circumstances played a part in his thought and responses, we must also acknowledge that Paul seems not always to have resolved the theological tensions inherent in his message or to have solved the practical difficulties involved in its application. When circumstances within the churches urged on him a more moderate course, he seems at times to have argued more from the categories of creation and curse than from the categories of eschatological redemption in Christ. At such times he appears, when judged from our present Christian perspective, almost chauvinistic. But we should not blame Paul too severely for failing to resolve all the tensions or solve all the difficulties, particularly since we seem to have done very little better in resolving them ourselves. On the contrary, we should applaud him for what he did do: he began to relate

[15]1 Tim. 2:12, "I do not permit a woman to teach or to have authority over a man," has usually been interpreted out of context. Catherine C. Kroeger's study of the verb *authentein* (here translated "to have authority") is significant, for she shows from then-current usage that the word connotes loose sexual behavior (as often practiced in the pagan cults) and that therefore the prohibition of 1 Tim. 2:12 should be seen as against Christian women imitating pagan female teachers who "made it evident in the course of their lectures that they were available afterwards for a second occupation" ("Ancient Heresies and a Strange Greek Verb," *The Reformed Journal,* March 1979, pp. 12–15). So in context, Paul commands Christian women—in contradistinction to the gross immorality of their pagan backgrounds—to dress modestly and with propriety (vv. 9–10), not to be seductresses (vv. 13–14), and to realize that their womanly instincts are fulfilled in giving birth to legitimate children (v. 15). Ms. Kroeger's thesis does not minimize Paul's admonitions that "a woman should learn in quietness and full submission" (v. 11) and that "she must be silent" (v. 12b). But it does provide an explanation for what has often appeared to be bizarre in the passage, and it provides us with a circumstantial rationale for the stress on submission and silence here.

the theological categories of creation and redemption, most often emphasizing the latter; and he began to apply the gospel principles of freedom, mutuality, and equality to the situations of his day—including that of the place and status of women. In so doing, he set a pattern and marked out a path for Christian thought and action after him to follow.

And first-century Christians seem, generally, to have been prepared to move forward on such a path. While the early Christian confession now incorporated at 1 Corinthians 15:3b–5 excludes the testimony of women, Mark's Gospel highlights their presence at Christ's crucifixion and entombment (15:40–41, 47) and their witness to Christ's resurrection (16:1–8). In fact, after the second great confession of his Gospel—namely, that of the Roman centurion declaring "Surely this man was the Son of God" (15:39; cf. Peter's of 8:29)—Mark focuses his readers' attention almost exclusively on the testimony of the women. Luke's Gospel also lays emphasis on women, both in its first two chapters, which portray Elizabeth's situation, Mary's response, and Anna's praise, and in its many subtle nuances throughout the common narrative. Perhaps most interesting in this regard are Luke's "pairing parables," in which he sets up Jesus' actions and words in a manner that treats first men and then women: healing a centurion's servant (7:2–10) and raising a widow's son (7:11–15); teaching a scribe about the meaning of neighborliness (10:25–37) and teaching Mary and Martha what is best in the kingdom of God (10:38–42); the parable of the shepherd and his lost sheep (15:3–7) and the parable of a woman and her lost coin (15:8–10).

In Acts, Luke continues this emphasis on women, referring not only to "the women and Mary" in the upper room (1:14) and Philip's "four unmarried daughters who had the gift of prophecy" (21:9), but also to such women as Lydia (16:14–15, 40) and Priscilla (18:2–3, 18–19, 26) as prominent figures in the Pauline churches. Likewise in John's Gospel it is women, so socially insignificant in ancient Judaism, who play a prominent part in the portrayal of the salvation story. Where men in the Fourth Gospel are characteristically asking for signs and opposing Jesus, women often minister to him—as when a Samaritan woman gives him water (4:4ff.); Mary of Bethany anoints him in preparation for his burial (12:3); and "his mother, his mother's sister, Mary the wife of Clopas, and Mary of Magdala" stay with him during the crucifixion (19:25; along with John "standing nearby," 19:26–27). It is to the Samaritan woman that Jesus first acknowledges his Messiahship (4:26); for the comfort of Martha and Mary that he raises their brother Lazarus from the dead (11:1–44); and to Mary of Magdala that he first appears after his resurrection (20:11–18). Such portrayals and patterns are not without significance. Their presence in the Gospels reflects a growing consciousness within the apostolic Church of the impact of the gospel on its attitude toward the importance and status of women.

D. THE CHURCH AND WOMEN IN SUCCEEDING CENTURIES

The relation of men and women in the Church during the Ante-Nicene period is a difficult topic, simply because there is so little written from the period that bears directly on the subject. The Greek Christian tradition provides only a few scattered hints; the Latin tradition supplies somewhat more information. Taking the sum total of evidence available, however, we are woefully short of anything like an adequate picture.

In the mid-second century, Montanus came to prominence in the region of Phrygia in Asia Minor as the leader of a heretical sect with eschatological and charismatic features. Sharing leadership with him were two women whom he converted to his persuasion, Maximilla and Prisca, who both claimed to be prophetesses. Eusebius in the fourth century wrote pejoratively about "Montanus and his women" (*Ecclesiastical History* 5.16), with his derisive tone clearly evident even in print. But there is no evidence that in the second century Montanists were rejected by more orthodox Christians because women had positions of leadership in the movement. It was rather the Montanists' doctrinal aberrations which separated them from catholic Christendom.

The third-century Greek *Didascalia Apostolorum* ("Teachings of the Apostles") describes in detail the duties of deacons and deaconesses, with the first office being confined to men and the second to women (ch. 16). But the descriptions give no sense that one office is unequal or inferior to the other. Only their respective duties are distinguished, for deaconesses were "to go into the houses of the heathen where there are believing women, and to visit those who are sick, and to minister to them in that of which they have need, and to bathe those who have begun to recover from sickness" (16.3).

In the Latin tradition, however, there appears a decided trend toward the subordination of women. Tertullian of Carthage, for example, writing about A.D. 202 *On the Apparel of Women*, says to Christian women:

> And do you not know that you are each Eve? The sentence of death on this sex of yours lives in this age: the guilt must of necessity live too. You are the devil's gateway; you are the unsealer of the forbidden tree; you are the first deserter of the divine law; you are she who persuaded him whom the devil was not valiant enough to attack. You destroyed God's image, man. On account of your desert—that is, death—even the Son of God had to die. (1.1)

Thus, as every wife was Eve, the seducer of Adam, she was to be subordinate and in submission to her husband. And with such a rationale, the theological categories of creation and curse became dominant over that of redemption.

With Jerome (A.D. 340–420), the theme of women as temptresses of men became fixed in the Latin church and the inferior position of women generally became established. Also through Jerome, whom J. N. D. Kelly calls "the champion of chastity,"[16] virginity and celibacy became elevated to the status of a more noble spirituality. The Western text of the Acts of the Apostles, for example, reflects his influence on the subject of women in four of its readings: (1) at 1:14, where it adds "and children" to the reference to "the women" in the upper room, thereby suggesting that these women were wives of the apostles and minimizing the independent activity of

---

[16]Kelly, *Jerome* (New York: Harper & Row, 1975), p. 106, n. 10. Jerome's struggles with his own sexual passions are well known, for he wrote of them quite freely (cf., e.g., *Letters* 22.7). In one of his letters he says that he took up the study of Hebrew because it was more useful than fasting for the restraining of sexual passion (cf. *Letters* 125).

women in that earliest Christian assembly; (2) at 17:12, where it recasts "many of the Jews believed, as did also a number of prominent Greek women and many Greek men" to read "also many of the Greeks, prominent men and women, believed," thereby reversing the order of women and men in the text; (3) at 17:34, where no mention is made of the woman Damaris as a convert at Athens; and (4) at 18:26, where the names Priscilla and Aquila are reversed to read "Aquila and Priscilla."

With Martin Luther, however, a more redemptive note regarding women was struck. Luther accepted the subordination of women to men because of their derivative creation. But he was not prepared to accept their inferiority to men because of the curse, nor to elevate virginity and celibacy to positions of greater spirituality. Rather, he viewed the combination of subordination because of creation and liberation because of redemption as producing what Roland Bainton calls a "domesticated womanhood"[17]—that is, a womanhood freed by redemption from the social effects of the curse and therefore able to fulfill its rightful place in the family. Thus, when speaking about God's punishment of Eve, Luther says:

> Therefore truly happy and joyful is this punishment if we correctly appraise the matter. Although these burdens are troublesome for the flesh, yet the hope for a better life is strengthened together with those very burdens or punishments, because Eve hears that she is not being repudiated by God. Furthermore, she also hears that in this punishment she is not being deprived of the blessing of procreation, which was promised and granted before sin. She sees that she is keeping her sex and that she remains a woman. She sees that she is not being separated from Adam to remain alone and apart from her husband. She sees that she may keep the glory of motherhood, if I may use the phrase. All these things are in addition to the eternal hope, and without a doubt they greatly encouraged Eve. Above all, there remains also a greater and more genuine glory. Not only does she keep the blessing of fruitfulness and remain united with her husband, but she has the sure promise that from her will come the Seed who will crush the head of Satan.[18]

[17]Bainton, *Here I Stand* (Nashville: Abingdon-Cokesbury, 1950), pp. 286–304.

[18]"Lectures on Genesis," in *Luther's Works*, vol. 1, ed. J. Pelikan (St. Louis: Concordia, 1958), 199.

Whereas the Latin church both put women down generally because of their derivative creation and their weakness to temptation, and elevated certain women because of their virginity, Luther saw in Genesis 2–3 and heard throughout the Scriptures the note of redemption. He still spoke of their subordination, but he viewed women and the relation of men and women differently than did Rome because of his emphasis on redemption and freedom in Christ—as his marriage to the former nun Katherine von Bora illustrates.

E. SOME IMPLICATIONS FOR TODAY

Though it is unpleasant to confess, it must in all honesty be said that there still exists among Christians today an attitude toward women which is, for the most part, a put-down. It is an attitude expressed directly in words, indirectly through tonal inflections, and by a variety of practices. It is particularly evident in the roles assigned to women in the Church and open to women in society. Often Paul is blamed for this put-down. But while Paul did not resolve the question of male-female relations, he went a good deal further in proposing a solution than we usually recognize.

At the heart of the problem as it exists in the Church is the question of how we correlate the theological categories of creation and redemption. Where the former is stressed, subordination and submission are usually emphasized—sometimes even silence; where the latter is stressed, freedom, mutuality, and equality are usually emphasized. What Paul attempted to do in working out his theology was to keep both categories united—though, I would insist, with an emphasis on redemption. Because of creation there are differences between the sexes which exist for the blessing of both men and women and for the benefit of society. Paul does not argue for anything like unisexuality or some supposed androgynous ideal. Heterosexuality is presupposed in all of his letters as having been ordained by God, and he has nothing but contempt and condemnation for homosexual practices. Yet Paul also lays emphasis on redemption in such a way as to indicate that what God has done in Christ transcends what is true simply because of creation.

Admittedly, Paul did not go as far himself with regard to the male-female question as he did with regard to the Jewish-Gentile problem, or even with regard to slavery. But in that Galatians 3:28 speaks of there being "neither Jew nor Greek, slave nor free, male nor female" in the new fellowship established by God in Christ Jesus, we may say that in the same way that Jews have no exclusive privilege over Gentiles and free persons no exclusive advantage over slaves, so men are to have no exclusive prerogatives over women. It is such a truth that Christians individually and the Church corporately need to express today if we are to work out a Christian social ethic that is based on the principles of the gospel and that follows the paradigm set by the apostolic practice.

EPILOGUE

Our purpose in this book has been primarily to offer an answer to the questions "How should the New Testament be used in areas of social concern?" and "Of what relevance are its pronouncements, principles, and practices for social ethics today?" In so doing, we have emphasized the hermeneutical dimensions of Christian ethics. And in dealing with hermeneutics, we have confined ourselves to investigations of the three couplets of Galatians 3:28—since it was in these areas that the early Christians faced their greatest problems socially, realized something of the significance of the gospel for their situations, and attempted to work out the implications of the gospel for their own day. The early Christians knew themselves to be "a kind of firstfruits" of God's new creation (Jas. 1:18; cf. Rom. 16:5b; 1 Cor. 16:15), and so sought (however hesitantly at times) to be God's people in truth and practice.

Today we face challenges that, although different from theirs, are in many ways the same. Racism, slavery, and sexism still haunt all of our human relationships (sadly, even in the Church), so that it is necessary to hear repeatedly the affirmations of that great Magna Carta of the Christian faith incorporated at Galatians 3:28 and to trace out as a paradigm for our lives the early Christian attempts to put those principles into practice. Yet it is also necessary to go beyond what those early Christians did explicitly and to ask regarding the relevance of the Christian message for all areas of our lives today—that is, with respect to such matters as poverty, ethnic minorities, political enslavement, genetic engineering, abortion, euthanasia, environmental contamination, labor-management relations, international relations, nuclear armaments, et al. While we have spoken only about New Testament social ethics in this book, our purpose has been to establish a basis and set a pattern for the much larger discussion of Christian social ethics.

Jesus, we are told, lived under the mandate of Isaiah 61:1–2a, and so saw his ministry as having both personal and social significance:

> "The Spirit of the Lord is on me;
>> therefore he has anointed me to preach good news to the poor.
> He has sent me to proclaim freedom for the prisoners
>> and recovery of sight for the blind,
> to release the oppressed,
>> to proclaim the year of the Lord's favor." (Luke 4:18–19)

And Jesus made it very clear that he expected his disciples to express their relationship with him in ways that would be both personally and socially relevant as well. In the Sermon on the Mount, for example, he began by saying:

> "You are the salt of the earth. But if the salt loses its saltiness, how can it be made salty again? It is no longer good for anything, except to be thrown out and trampled by men.
> "You are the light of the world. A city on a hill cannot be hidden. Neither do people light a lamp and put it under a bowl. Instead they put it on its stand, and it gives light to everyone in the house. In the same way, let your light shine before men, that they may see your good deeds and praise your Father in heaven." (Matt. 5:13–16)

And in his last recorded parable he spoke of acceptance by God as being based on feeding the hungry, giving drink to the thirsty, welcoming the stranger, clothing the needy, looking after the sick, and visiting those in prison:

> " 'For I was hungry and you gave me something to eat, I was thirsty and you gave me something to drink, I was a stranger and you invited me in, I needed clothes and you clothed me, I was sick and you looked after me, I was in prison and you came to visit me.'
> "Then the righteous will answer him, 'Lord, when did we see you hungry and feed you, or thirsty and give you something to drink? When did we see you a stranger and invite you in, or needing clothes and clothe you? When did we see you sick or in prison and go to visit you?'

"The King will reply, 'I tell you the truth, whatever you did for one of the least of these brothers of mine, you did for me.' " (Matt. 25:35–40)

So Christians individually and the Church corporately— taking also as our motto the words of Isaiah 61:1–2a, in obedience to our Lord's commands, seeking to express the principles of the Christian gospel, and in line with the paradigm set by the earliest believers in Jesus—are called upon to live out our new life "in Christ" in ways that are both personally and socially relevant. As was Israel during the time of the Old Covenant, so the Church of the New Covenant is the primary social structure for the expression of God's reign. It is the arena wherein God's reign is to be most fully at work, and it is the instrument through which God's reign is to be most adequately expressed to an alien world. It is important as an instrument for the conversion of individuals. It is also important as the prototype for that new realm of social existence which God is calling into being. Its very presence in the world, like salt and light, has a salutary effect, both in condemning evil and in drawing people to Christ. But it also, again like salt and light, is meant to have an outreach and mission to the world—one that seeks to undercut evil and establish justice. To change the metaphor somewhat, the Israelites' mission was to be both centripetal (i.e., directed inward toward a central axis) and centrifugal (i.e., directed away from a central axis), though, sadly, they often emphasized the first to the exclusion of the second. The Church's mission is likewise to be both centripetal and centrifugal in nature, and it is ours as Christians individually and the Church corporately to hold the two in tandem.

All too often, Christians see redemption in Christ as something to be actively pursued and passively possessed. But the Good News proclaimed by the New Testament is that God redeems freely and bestows new life as a gift—with the result that becoming new creatures in Christ Jesus by faith, we are then and there called to a life of active participation with God by the power of his Spirit in the expression of that relationship. Faith in Christ is meant to be the basis for a life of expanded vision, sharpened sensitivities, moral courage, and active endeavor, not a substitute for thought or change.

True faith in Christ, Paul says, is always actively "expressing itself through love" (Gal. 5:6; cf. also vv. 13–15). So the apostle closes his letter to the Galatians with words that need to resound continually in our hearts and minds as well: "Therefore, as we have opportunity, let us do good to all people, especially to those who belong to the family of believers" (6:10).

A SELECTED BIBLIOGRAPHY FOR FURTHER STUDY

A. ON NEW TESTAMENT THEOLOGY TODAY
(for Introduction):

Achtemeier, P., and G. M. Tucker. "Biblical Studies: The State of the Discipline." *Bulletin of the Council on the Study of Religion*, 11 (1980), 72–76.

Barr, James. "Trends and Prospects in Biblical Theology." *Journal of Theological Studies*, 25 (1974), 265–82.

Bruce, F. F. "Charting New Directions for New Testament Studies." *Christianity Today*, 24 (1980), 1117–20.

Crossan, J. Domenic. "Perspectives and Methods in Contemporary Biblical Criticism." *Biblical Research*, 22 (1977), 39–49.

Dahl, Nils A. "New Testament Theology in a Pluralistic Setting." *Reflection*, 77 (1980), 16–18.

Fuller, Reginald H. "The New Testament in Current Study." *Perspectives in Religious Studies*, 1 (1974), 103–19.

_____. "What is Happening in New Testament Studies?" *Saint Luke's Journal of Theology*, 23 (1980), 90–100.

Kaye, B. N. "Recent German Roman Catholic New Testament Research." *Churchman*, 89 (1975), 246–56.

Kistemaker, Simon J. "Current Problems and Projects in New Testament Research." *Journal of the Evangelical Theological Society*, 71 (1975), 17–28.

Martin, Ralph P. "New Testament Theology: Impasse and Exit. The Issues." *The Expository Times*, 91 (1980), 264–69.

Pfitzner, V. C. "Pointers to New Testament Studies Today." *Lutheran Theological Journal*, 13 (1979), 7–14.

Riesenfeld, Harald. "Criteria and Valuations in Biblical Studies." *Svensk Exegetisk Arsbok*, 39 (1974), 74–89.

Robinson, James M. "The Future of New Testament Theology." *Religious Studies Review*, 2 (1976), 17–23.

Scroggs, Robin. "The Sociological Interpretation of the New Testament: The Present State of Research." *New Testament Studies*, 26 (1980), 164–79.

Stuhlmacher, Peder. "The Gospel of Reconciliation in Christ—Basic Features and Issues of a Biblical Theology of the New Testament." *Horizons in Biblical Theology*, 1 (1979), 161–90.

B. ON THE USE OF THE NEW TESTAMENT IN ETHICS (for Chapter I):

Brunner, Emil. *The Divine Imperative: A Study in Christian Ethics.* Trans. O. Wyon. London: Lutterworth, 1937.

Dodd, C. H. *Gospel and Law: The Relation of Faith and Ethics in Early Christianity.* Cambridge: Cambridge University Press, 1951.

Fletcher, Joseph. *Situation Ethics: The New Morality.* Philadelphia: Westminister Press, 1966.

Furnish, Victor Paul. *Theology and Ethics in Paul.* Nashville: Abingdon Press, 1968.

Gardner, E. Clinton. *Biblical Faith and Social Ethics.* New York: Harper & Row, 1960.

Gustafson, James M. *The Church as Moral Decision-Maker.* Philadelphia: Pilgrim: 1970.

————. "The Place of Scripture in Christian Ethics, a Methodological Study." *Interpretation*, 24 (1970), 430–55.

Henry, Carl F. H. *Aspects of Christian Social Ethics.* Grand Rapids, Mich.: Eerdmans, 1964.

————. *Christian Personal Ethics.* Grand Rapids, Mich.: Eerdmans, 1957.

Hiers, Richard H. *Jesus and Ethics, Four Interpretations.* Philadelphia: Westminster Press, 1968.

Houlden, J. L. *Ethics and the New Testament.* New York: Oxford University Press, 1973.

Kahn, Robert I. *The Letter and the Spirit.* Waco, Texas: Word, 1972.

Knox, John. *The Ethic of Jesus in the Teaching of the Church: Its Authority and Its Relevance.* New York: Abingdon Press, 1961.

Lehmann, Paul. *Ethics in a Christian Context.* New York: Harper & Row, 1963.

Long, Edward LeRoy, Jr. "The Use of the Bible in Christian Ethics, A Look at Basic Options." *Interpretation*, 19 (1965), 149–62.

Longenecker, Richard N. *Paul, Apostle of Liberty.* New York: Harper & Row, 1964 (esp. pp. 128–208).

Muilenburg, James. *The Way of Israel: Biblical Faith and Ethics.* New York: Harper, 1961.

Murray, John. *Principles of Conduct: Aspects of Biblical Ethics.* Grand Rapids, Mich.: Eerdmans, 1957.

Niebuhr, H. Richard. *Christ and Culture*. New York: Harper & Row, 1951.

Niebuhr, Reinhold. *An Interpretation of Christian Ethics*. New York: Harper, 1935.

_____. *Moral Man and Immoral Society*. New York: Scribner's, 1934.

Nineham, Dennis. *The Use and Abuse of the Bible: The Study of the Bible in an Age of Rapid Cultural Change*. London: Macmillan, 1976.

Ramsey, Paul. "The Biblical Norm of Righteousness." *Interpretation*, 24 (1970), 419–29.

Sanders, Jack T. *Ethics in the New Testament: Change and Development*. Philadelphia: Fortress Press, 1975.

Schnackenburg, Rudolf. *The Moral Teaching of the New Testament*. Trans. J. Holland-Smith and W. J. O'Hara. New York: Herder & Herder, 1965.

Sittler, Joseph. *The Structure of Christian Ethics*. Baton Rouge: Louisiana State University Press, 1958.

C. ON A DEVELOPMENT HERMENEUTIC (for Chapter II):

Brown, Raymond E. *The "Sensus Plenior" of Holy Scripture*. Baltimore: St. Mary's University, 1955.

Chadwick, Owen. *From Bousset to Newman: The Idea of Doctrinal Development*. London: Cambridge University Press, 1957.

Dunn, James G. *Unity and Diversity in the New Testament*. London: SCM, 1977.

Geiselmann, J. R. *Die katholische Tübinger Schule. Ihre theologische Eigenart*. Freiburg: Herder, 1964.

Harnack, Adolf. *Lehrbuch der Dogmengeschichte*. Freiburg: Mohr, 1886 (one-volume abridgement: *Outlines of the History of Dogma*. Trans. E. K. Mitchell. London: Hodder & Stoughton, 1893).

Lonergan, Bernard J. F. *Method in Theology*. New York: Herder & Herder, 1972.

Longenecker, Richard N. *Biblical Exegesis in the Apostolic Period*. Grand Rapids, Mich.: Eerdmans, 1975.

_____. "The Obedience of Christ in the Theology of the Early Church." In *Reconciliation and Hope* (Leon L. Morris *Festschrift*). Ed. R. Banks. Grand Rapids, Mich.: Eerdmans, 1974, pp. 142–52.

_____. "On the Concept of Development in Pauline Thought." In *Perspectives on Evangelical Theology*. Ed. K. S. Kantzer and S. N. Gundry. Grand Rapids, Mich.: Baker, 1979, pp. 195–207.

Marshall, I. Howard. " 'Early Catholicism' in the New Testament." In *New Dimensions in New Testament Study*. Ed. R. N. Longenecker and M. C. Tenney. Grand Rapids, Mich.: Zondervan, 1974, pp. 217–31.

Marxsen, Willi. *Der "Frühkatholizismus" im Neuen Testament.* Neu-kirchen: Neukirchener Verlag, 1964.

Moran, Gabriel. *Theology of Revelation.* New York: Herder & Herder, 1966.

Newman, John Henry. *An Essay on the Development of Christian Doctrine.* London: Toovey, 1845.

Orr, James. *The Progress of Dogma.* London: Hodder & Stoughton, 1901.

Pelikan, Jaroslav. *The Christian Tradition: A History of the Development of Doctrine.* 2 vols. Chicago: University of Chicago Press, 1971–1974.

————. *Development of Christian Doctrine: Some Historical Phenomena.* New Haven, Conn.: Yale University Press, 1969.

————. *Historical Theology: Continuity and Change in Christian Doctrine.* Philadelphia: Westminster Press, 1971.

Rahner, Karl. *Theological Investigations.* Vols. 1, 4. Trans. C. Ernst. Baltimore: Helicon, 1961, 1966.

Rainy, Robert. *The Delivery and Development of Christian Doctrine.* Edinburgh: T. & T. Clark, 1874.

Sabatier, Auguste. *The Apostle Paul: A Sketch of the Development of His Doctrine.* Trans. A. M. Hellier. London: Hodder & Stoughton, 1896.

Toon, Peter. *The Development of Doctrine in the Church.* Grand Rapids, Mich.: Eerdmans, 1979.

Vos, Geerhardus. *Biblical Theology.* Grand Rapids, Mich.: Eerdmans, 1948.

Warfield, Benjamin B. "The Idea of Systematic Theology." In *Studies in Theology.* New York: Oxford University Press, 1932.

Wiles, Maurice F. *The Making of Christian Doctrine.* New York: Cambridge University Press, 1967.

————. *The Remaking of Christian Doctrine.* London: SCM, 1974.

D. ON JEWS AND GENTILES IN CHRIST
(for Chapter III):

Baum, Gregory. *Is the New Testament Anti-Semitic?* Green Rock, N.J.: Paulist Press, 1965 (repr. of *The Jews and the Gospel*, 1961).

Bratton, Fred G. *The Crime of Christendom: The Theological Sources of Christian Anti-Semitism.* Boston: Beacon Press, 1969.

Bromiley, Geoffrey W. "Who Says the New Testament is Anti-Semitic?" *Christianity Today,* 11 (1966–67), 548–49.

Crossan, J. Domenic. "Anti-Semitism and the Gospel." *Theological Studies,* 26 (1965), 189–215.

Davies, Alan T. *Anti-Semitism and the Christian Mind*. New York: Herder & Herder, 1969.

—————, ed. *Anti-Semitism and the Foundations of Christianity*. New York: Paulist Press, 1979.

Davies, W. D. "Paul and the People of Israel." *New Testament Studies*, 24 (1977), 4–39.

DeLange, N. R. M. *Origen and the Jews: Studies in Jewish-Christian Relations in Third-Century Palestine*. Cambridge: Cambridge University Press, 1976.

Grant, Frederick C. *Ancient Judaism and the New Testament*. New York: Macmillan, 1959.

Isaac, Jules. *Genese de l'antisémitisme*. Paris: Calmann-Levy, 1956.

—————. *Jesus and Israel*. Trans. S. Gran. New York: Holt, Rinehart, and Winston, 1971.

Jocz, Jakob. *The Jewish People and Jesus Christ*. London: S.P.C.K., 1949.

—————. *The Jewish People and Jesus Christ After Auschwitz: A Study in the Controversy Between Church and Synagogue*. Grand Rapids, Mich.: Baker, 1981.

Katz, Jacob. *Exclusiveness and Tolerance: Studies in Jewish-Gentile Relations in Medieval and Modern Times*. London: Oxford University Press, 1961.

Parkes, James. *The Conflict of the Church and the Synagogue*. London: Soncino, 1934.

—————. *A History of the Jewish People*. London: Weidenfeld and Nicolson, 1962.

—————. *Jesus, Paul, and the Jews*. London: SCM, 1936.

—————. *Judaism and Christianity*. Chicago: University of Chicago Press, 1948.

—————. *Prelude to Dialogue: Jewish-Christian Relationships*. New York: Schocken, 1969.

Richardson, Peter. *Israel in the Apostolic Church*. Cambridge: Cambridge University Press, 1969.

—————. *Paul's Ethic of Freedom*. Philadelphia: Westminster Press, 1979.

Ruether, Rosemary R. *Faith and Fratricide: The Theological Roots of Anti-Semitism*. New York: Seabury Press, 1974.

Sandmel, Samuel. *Anti-Semitism in the New Testament?* Philadelphia: Fortress Press, 1978.

Schoeps, Hans J. *The Jewish-Christian Agreement: A History of Theologies in Conflict*. Trans. D. E. Green. London: Faber & Faber, 1963.

Stendahl, Krister. *Paul Among Jews and Gentiles*. Philadelphia: Fortress Press, 1976.

Wilde, Robert. *The Treatment of the Jews in the Greek Christian Writers of the First Three Centuries*. Washington, D.C.: Catholic University Press, 1949.

E. ON SLAVERY AND FREEDOM IN CHRIST
(for Chapter IV):

Barrow, Reginald H. *Slavery in the Roman Empire*. London: Methuen, 1928.

Bartchy, S. Scott. *Mallon Chrēsai: First-Century Slavery and the Interpretation of I Corinthians 7:21*. Cambridge, Mass.: Society of Biblical Literature, 1973.

Daube, David. "Slave Catching." *Juridical Review*, 64 (1952), 12–28.

Finley, Moses I., ed. *Slavery in Classical Antiquity: Views and Controversies*. Cambridge: Heffer, 1960.

Jewish Encyclopedia, s.v. "Slaves and Slavery."

Jones, A. H. M. "Slavery in the Ancient World." *Economic History Review*, 9 (1956), 185–99 (also included in Finley's symposium above).

————. *Studies in Roman Government and Law*. New York: Praeger, 1960.

Käsemann, Ernst. *Jesus Means Freedom*. Trans. F. Clarke. Philadelphia: Fortress Press, 1970.

Koch, Eldon W. "A Cameo of Koinonia: The Letter to Philemon." *Interpretation*, 17 (1963), 183–87.

Lillie, William. "The Pauline House Tables." *The Expository Times*, 86 (1975), 179–83.

Longenecker, Richard N. *Paul, Apostle of Liberty*. New York: Harper & Row, 1964.

Luther, Martin. "The Freedom of a Christian." *Luther's Works*, 31, ed. H. T. Lehmann. St. Louis: Concordia, 1957, 343–77.

Lyall, F. "Roman Law in the Writings of Paul—The Slave and the Freedman." *New Testament Studies*, 17 (1970), 73–79.

Mendelsohn, Isaac. *Slavery in the Ancient Near East*. New York: Oxford University Press, 1949.

Preiss, Theo. "Life in Christ and Social Ethics in the Epistle to Philemon." In *Life in Christ*. London: SCM, 1954, pp. 32–42.

Richardson, Peter. *Paul's Ethic of Freedom*. Philadelphia: Westminster Press, 1979.

Richardson, William J. "Principle and Context in the Ethics of the Epistle to Philemon." *Interpretation*, 22 (1968), 301–16.

Rostovstev, Mikhail I. *The Social and Economic History of the Roman Empire*. Oxford: Clarendon, 1926.

Rupprecht, Arthur A. "Attitudes on Slavery Among the Church Fathers." In *New Dimensions in New Testament Study*. Ed. R. N. Longenecker and M. C. Tenney. Grand Rapids, Mich.: Zondervan, 1974, pp. 261–77.

_____. "Christianity and the Slavery Question." *Bulletin of the Evangelical Theological Society*, 6 (1963), 64–68.

Schultz, S. "Hat Christus die Sklaven befreit? Sklaverei und Emanzipationsbewegungen im Abendland." *Evangelische Kommentare*, 5 (1972), 13–17.

Schweizer, Eduard. "Traditional Ethical Patterns in the Pauline and Post-Pauline Letters and Their Development (List of Vices and House-Tables)." In *Text and Interpretation* (Matthew Black *Festschrift*). Ed. E. Best and R. McL. Wilson. Cambridge: Cambridge University Press, 1979, pp. 195–209.

_____. "Zum Sklavenproblem in Neuen Testament." *Evangelische Theologie*, 32 (1972), 502–06.

Westermann, William L. *The Slave Systems of Greek and Roman Antiquity*. Philadelphia: American Philosophical Society, 1955.

Wiedemann, T. *Greek and Roman Slavery*. Baltimore: Johns Hopkins University Press, 1981.

Wood, A. S. "Social Involvement in the Apostolic Church." *Evangelical Quarterly*, 42 (1970), 194–212.

Zeitlin, Solomon. "Slavery During the Second Commonwealth and Tannaitic Period." *Jewish Quarterly Review*, 53 (1962–63), 185–218.

F. ON MEN AND WOMEN IN CHRIST (for Chapter V):

Bainton, Roland H. *Women of the Reformation in Germany and Italy*. Minneapolis, Minn.: Augsburg, 1977.

Boldrey, Richard and Joyce. *Chauvinist or Feminist? Paul's View of Women*. Grand Rapids, Mich.: Baker, 1976.

Carmichael, Calum M. *Women, Law, and the Genesis Traditions*. Edinburgh: Edinburgh University Press, 1979.

Clemens, Lois Gunden. *Women Liberated*. Scottdale, Pa.: Herald Press, 1971.

Faxon, Alicia Craig. *Women and Jesus*. Philadelphia: United Church Press, 1973.

Furnish, Victor Paul. *The Moral Teaching of Paul: Selected Issues*. Nashville: Abingdon Press, 1979.

Gryson, R. *The Ministry of Women in the Early Church*. Trans. J. Laporte and M. L. Hall. Collegeville, Minn.: Liturgical Press, 1976.

Harkness, Georgia. *Women in Church and Society*. Nashville: Abingdon Press, 1972.

Harper, Joyce. *Women and the Gospel*. Pinner, England: Christian Brethren Research Fellowship, 1974.

Jewett, Paul King. *Man as Male and Female*. Grand Rapids, Mich.: Eerdmans, 1975.

———. *The Ordination of Women*. Grand Rapids, Mich.: Eerdmans, 1980.

Knight, George W., III. *The New Testament Teaching on the Role Relationships of Men and Women*. Grand Rapids, Mich.: Baker, 1977.

Lefkowitz, Mary R., and Maureen B. Fant. *Women in Greece and Rome*. Toronto: Samuel-Stevens, 1977.

Leipoldt, J. *Die Frau in der antiken Welt und im Urchristentum*. Leipzig: Koehler & Amelang, 1955.

Loewe, Raphael. *The Position of Women in Judaism*. London: S.P.C.K., 1966.

Meeks, Wayne A. "The Image of the Androgyne: Some Uses of a Symbol in Earliest Christinity." *History of Religions*, 13 (1974), 165–208.

Mollenkott, Virginia Ramey. *Women, Men and the Bible*. Nashville: Abingdon Press, 1977.

Neusner, Jacob. "Women in the System of Mishnah." *Conservative Judaism*, 33 (1980), 3–13.

Pape, Dorothy. *God and Women: A Fresh Look at What the New Testament Says about Women*. Oxford: Mowbrays, 1978.

Richardson, Peter. *Paul's Ethic of Freedom*. Philadelphia: Westminster Press, 1979.

Ruether, Rosemary R., and Eleanor McLaughlin, ed. *Women of Spirit: Female Leadership in the Jewish and Christian Traditions*. New York: Simon & Schuster, 1979.

Scroggs, Robin. "Paul and the Eschatological Woman." *Journal of the American Academy of Religion*, 40 (1972), 283–303.

Seltman, Charles T. *Women in Antiquity*. New York: Collier, 1962.

Stendahl, Krister. *The Bible and the Role of Women*. Trans. E. T. Sander. Philadelphia: Fortress Press, 1966.

Swidler, Leonard. *Women in Judaism: The Status of Women in Formative Judaism*. Metuchen, N.J.: Scarecrow Press, 1976.

Tavard, George H. *Women in Christian Tradition*. Notre Dame, Ind.: University of Notre Dame Press, 1973.

Tetlow, Elizabeth M. *Women and Ministry in the New Testament*. New York: Paulist Press, 1980.

Williams, D. *The Apostle Paul and Women in the Church*. Van Nuys, Calif.: BIM Pub., 1977.

G. TOWARD A CHRISTIAN SOCIAL ETHIC
(for Epilogue):

Bennett, John C. *Christian Ethics and Social Policy*. New York: Scribner's, 1946.

————, ed. *Christian Social Ethics in a Changing World*. New York: Association, 1966.

————. *Social Salvation: A Religious Approach to the Problems of Social Change*. New York: Scribner's, 1935.

Berkhof, Hendrikus. *Christ and the Powers*. Scottdale, Pa.: Herald Press, 1962.

Birch, Bruce C., and Larry L. Rasmussen. *Bible and Ethics in the Christian Life*. Minneapolis, Minn.: Augsburg, 1976.

Brown, Dale W. *The Christian Revolutionary*. Grand Rapids, Mich.: Eerdmans, 1971.

Brunner, Emil. *Justice and the Social Order*. London: Lutterworth, 1945.

Christenson, Larry. *A Charismatic Approach to Social Action*. Minneapolis, Minn.: Bethany Fellowship, 1974.

Cone, James H. *God of the Oppressed*. New York: Seabury Press, 1975.

Curran, Charles E. *Politics, Medicine, and Christian Ethics*. Philadelphia: Fortress Press, 1973.

Davies, J. G. *Christians, Politics and Violent Revolution*. London: SCM, 1976.

Ellul, Jacques. *The Political Illusion*. New York: Vintage Books, 1965.

Gill, Athol. "Christian Social Responsibility." In *The New Face of Evangelicalism: An International Symposium on the Lausanne Covenant*. Ed. C. R. Padilla. Downers Grove, Ill.: Inter-Varsity Press, 1976.

Gustafson, James M. *Christ and the Moral Life*. New York: Harper & Row, 1968.

————, ed. *The Church as Moral Decision-Maker*. Philadelphia: Pilgrim, 1970.

Henry, Carl F. H. *Aspects of Christian Social Ethics*. Grand Rapids, Mich.: Eerdmans, 1964.

Hutchison, J., ed. *Christian Faith and Social Action*. New York: Scribner's, 1953.

Kerans, Patrick. *Sinful Social Structures*. New York: Paulist Press, 1974.

Lehmann, Paul. *The Transformation of Politics*. New York: Harper, 1975.

Moberg, David O. *The Great Reversal: Evangelism versus Social Concern*. Philadelphia: Lippincott, 1972.

Mott, Stephen C. *Biblical Ethics and Social Change*. New York: Oxford University Press, 1982.

Mouw, Richard J. *Political Evangelism*. Grand Rapids, Mich.: Eerdmans, 1973.

————. *Politics and the Biblical Drama*. Grand Rapids, Mich.: Eerdmans, 1976.

Niebuhr, Reinhold. *Christian Realism and Political Problems*. New York: Scribner's, 1953.

————. *Moral Man and Immoral Society*. New York: Scribner's, 1932.

Outka, Gene. *"Agape": An Ethical Analysis*. New Haven, Conn.: Yale University Press, 1972.

Ramsey, Paul. *Basic Christian Ethics*. New York: Scribner's, 1950.

Rasmussen, Albert. *Christian Social Ethics*. Englewood Cliffs, N.J.: Prentice-Hall, 1956.

Rauschenbusch, Walter. *Christianity and the Social Crisis*. Boston: Pilgrim, 1907.

Ruether, Rosemary R. *Radical Social Movement and the Radical Church Tradition*. Oak Brook, Ill.: Bethany Theological Seminary, 1971.

Sider, Ronald J. *Christ and Violence*. Scottdale, Pa.: Herald Press, 1979.

————, ed. *Cry Justice! The Bible on Hunger and Poverty*. New York: Paulist Press, 1980.

————. *Rich Christians in an Age of Hunger*. Downers Grove, Ill.: Inter-Varsity Press, 1977.

Smith, Timothy L. *Revivalism and Social Reform in Mid-Nineteenth Century America*. New York: Abingdon Press, 1957.

Troeltsch, Ernst. *The Social Teachings of the Christian Churches*. New York: Harper, 1960.

Wallis, Jim. *Agenda for Biblical People*. New York: Harper & Row, 1976.

Webber, Robert E. *The Secular Saint: A Case for Evangelical Social Responsibility*. Grand Rapids, Mich.: Zondervan, 1979.

Wilder, Amos N. *Eschatology and Ethics in the Teaching of Jesus*. New York: Harper, 1939.

————. *Kerygma, Eschatology, and Social Ethics*. Philadelphia: Fortress Press, 1966.

Williams, Daniel D. *The Spirit and the Forms of Love*. New York: Harper & Row, 1968.

Yoder, John H. *The Christian Witness to the State*. Newton, Kans.: Faith and Life, 1964.

————, ed. *The Original Revolution*. Scottdale, Pa.: Herald Press, 1972.

————. *The Politics of Jesus*. Grand Rapids, Mich.: Eerdmans, 1972.